Also By Jennifer Holik

*Stories from the Battlefield: A Beginning Guide to World War II Research*

*Stories of the Lost*

*Engaging the Next Generation: A Guide for Genealogy Societies and Libraries*

*Branching Out: Genealogy for Adults*

*Branching Out: Genealogy for High School Students*

*Branching Out: Genealogy for 4th-8th Grades Students*

*Branching Out: Genealogy for 1st-3rd Grade Students*

*To Soar with the Tigers*

# The Tiger's Widow

A Woman Who Took Up the Fight, the Story of Virginia Brouk

Written by Jennifer Holik

Generations Publishing

Copyright Information

Copyright © 2014 Jennifer Holik
Publisher: Generations, Woodridge, Illinois

All rights reserved. This book, or parts thereof, may not be reproduced in any manner or form without written permission from the copyright holder and Virginia S. Davis or her heirs.

Editor: Heather Gates Reed

Cover Designer: Sarah Sucansky

Holik, Jennifer, 1973 –
 The Tiger's Widow / Jennifer Holik. Includes bibliographical references and indexes.

ISBN: 1500284599
ISBN-13: 978-1500284596

Printed in the United States of America

# Dedication

This book is dedicated with love to Virginia S. Davis, the late Robert Brouk, the late Fred Davis, and the late Harvey Davis. Thank you for all the love and lessons taught.

# Acknowledgements

This book could not have been written without the support of several people. First to Virginia S. Davis for sharing her heart and memories with me so I could write her incredible story. This remarkable, amazing woman has taught me more lessons than she knows.

Thank you to my boys who patiently listened to me talk about Ginny and all our family's military stories. Through you our family's stories will live on.

Thank you to my cover designer Sarah Sucansky, and outstanding editor Heather Gates Reed. All of my books could not come to fruition without your expertise.

To Norm Richards, a historian for the 90th Division Association, many thanks for helping me locate records at the National Personnel Records Center and answering every question I ever asked about military records. He is always and continues to be a wealth of information.

A big thank you to staff at the Pritzker Military Museum and Library in Chicago, Illinois. I'd like to thank Teri Embrey, Chief Librarian, and Paul Grasmehr, Reference Coordinator, for their assistance and support as I wrote and revised this story.

# Table of Contents

| | |
|---|---|
| Prologue | 13 |
| 1 Five Hearts Joined Together | 14 |
| 2 Ginny | 16 |
| 3 Hello Charley! | 19 |
| 4 Two Hearts Join | 29 |
| 5 The Final Flight | 38 |
| 6 The Decision to Join the Fight | 43 |
| 7 Ginny's WAAC Experience | 48 |
| 8 Going Overseas | 72 |
| 9 Finding Love Again | 118 |
| 10 Harvey and Ginny's Courtship | 122 |
| 11 Five Hearts Connected | 131 |
| Endnotes | 135 |
| Bibliography | 141 |
| Index | 144 |
| About The Author | 146 |

# Prologue

The second volume in the Stories of the Lost series is the story of one woman who made a difference in the war and the future of women, including me. Virginia Brouk heeded the call to arms and through her actions, allowed women of future generations to have more options than perhaps we would have if the war had not been fought.

This book highlights the Women's Army Corps (WAC) career of Virginia (Ginny) Brouk, the widow of Flying Tiger Robert Brouk. The story is not meant to recreate the entire history of the Women's Army Corps. That history has been written. Please see the bibliography for suggested reading.

Much of what is included in this volume was written by Ginny's hand in her memoir, letters we exchanged, or thoughts provided to me through oral history interviews. All the photographs are hers unless otherwise specified. The slang or wording spoken in the 1940s has been left in her words and has not been changed. You will see one word in particular, "WOG" which stood for Westernized Oriental Gentleman. Today this is seen as an offensive term, but in the 1940s it was commonly used and accepted. The presence of this word or others in this volume is not meant to cause offense, simply reflect the times in which they were used.

In keeping with the theme of "Lost" in this series, this volume invites you to discover what Ginny lost as a result of Robert's death and what she gained as she continued through the months afterward.

Thank you for sharing Ginny's story with me.

# 1
# Five Hearts Joined Together

Love knows no boundaries of time and space or life and death. It exists forever in our hearts as we remember and honor those who have gone before us. Through those memories we pass life lessons on to the next generation. We teach others there is light after darkness, hope after despair, and love is the glue that puts shattered hearts back together. This is a story of five hearts separated by time and space; hearts which would meet in the perfect moment. It is a story about never ending love that lived on even after death.

A famous pilot met a young beauty and the two fell in love, Robert and Ginny. Their love soared with the eagles. Their time together was brief but they lived so fully in love in the moment, it is as if nothing but death could have broken them apart. Then death knocked on their door and a plane fell from the sky in a fiery ball. One heart silenced on earth but lived forever in death. One heart shattered into a million pieces.

A year later on another continent, two brothers fought a war, Harvey and Fred. The boys grew up as orphans and wanted a heart to come home to. Fred flew a bombing mission over Austria and was lost, listed as missing for a year. Harvey feared the worst and waited for word which came a year after Fred went missing. A brother's love lived on after death.

Less than a year after Fred went missing, Ginny found Harvey. A chance meeting and two hearts became one. Pieces of Ginny's shattered heart started to glue back together, slowly at first and then more quickly. Harvey's heart had finally found its home with Ginny. He was no longer an orphan or alone. They found each other during a time of war when the world around them collapsed in chaos. Together they created a new world filled with joy, love, and the memories of those lost before their time.

Almost 65 years later, another heart emerged. A young woman trying to start a new life after her heart was shattered. She and Ginny, now a widow for the second time, connected. Little did they know the impact that meeting would have.

Five hearts separated by time and space that met in perfect time, would change the lives of all they touched. Their love would span decades. Their life lessons would provide hope to others in the future.

Five hearts joined forever.

# 2

# Ginny

Virginia (Ginny) was born on April 5, 1922 in Evanston, Illinois to Oscar and Frieda, nee Bigler, Scharer.[1] Oscar and Frieda were Swiss immigrants. Virginia also had a younger sister, Ruth Viola Scharer, born on May 3, 1925 in Chicago.[2]

*Ginny, Oscar, Frieda, and baby Ruth.*

The world Ginny was born into changed dramatically from her birth until the start of World War II. In those early years, the U.S. enjoyed prosperity and then plunged into a financial crisis like the country had never seen, The Great Depression.

The Depression lasted into the mid-1940s. Everyone learned to tighten their belts and save anything that might be useful for the family in future days. Families learned to ration household items and survive on a shoestring budget. Some families had to learn to function without the head of the household. Often, the father would travel from town to town looking for work to support his family when jobs were unavailable at home. The country did not know then these practices would serve them well when the U.S. joined the war on December 7, 1941.

*Ginny and Ruth circa 1926.*

Ginny and Ruthie grew from babies to young women during these tumultuous years supported by the firm family values of their parents. Ginny's father Oscar was a very protective and quiet man who did not rock the boat. He did not like a lot of attention drawn to him or the family so he did his best to ensure each

*The Scharer family in 1938. Frieda, Oscar, Ginny, and Ruthie.*

family member was humble and did their best. Under the guidance of both parents, the girls blossomed into wholesome young women who understood the value of stability, honor, pride, trust, and most importantly, love. It was out of this environment that Ginny became an incredible young woman and grew into a courageous, strong woman who served her country and rose up after tragedy to love again.

Ginny graduated from Steinmetz High School in Chicago in 1940. After graduation, Ginny worked for Collier Magazine and was a freelance model after having attended classes at Vera Janes Studios in Chicago. The job at Collier Magazine required Ginny to take the "L" to work from her home. Ginny's father grew concerned about his beautiful daughter traveling alone and helped get her a new job at the Hawthorne Works Western Electric Plant in Cicero, Illinois. Western Electric, a current-day subsidiary of AT&T Bell Telephone Company, was where her father had been employed as a mechanical engineer and tool designer for many years. In those days, if a family had a car, usually they would have only one. This enabled Ginny and her father the opportunity to bond while driving back and forth to work together. No longer would Oscar have to worry about Ginny on the "L."

Western Electric was unique in that it was situated on a large piece of land which held several major buildings and functioned like a small town. It contained Albright Memorial Field, a gymnasium, a restaurant, and theater. A small railroad ran through the complex to easily transport goods from the factories to the nearby Burlington Northern Santa Fe rail line.

Prior to the war, the company manufactured telephone equipment primarily. Once the U.S. entered the war, production changed some things changed as the company supported the war effort increasing the production of cables, telephone equipment, switchboards, and radios for infantry and Air Corps use. All of these pieces of equipment were quickly manufactured and shipped overseas for use.

Ginny was employed as an order clerk at Western Electric, a job which required her to place orders for parts and calculate numbers all day. Ginny was an excellent typist and preferred that type of office work to number crunching. However, her daily duties were soon to change.

*A page from Ginny's scrapbook.*

# 3
# Hello Charley!

In the 1920s, Western Electric had an employee named Charles Drucker. A postcard addressed to "Charley the Western ," was sent to the plant. It was intended for Charles Drucker, but the sender could not remember Charles' last name. As the postcard circulated the plant searching for the proper owner, plant workers started calling each other "Charley Western" which became "Hello Charley" as a greeting. In 1930, the company used the "Hello Charley" greeting to create a beauty pageant and crowned the first "Hello Charley" girl.

The "Hello Charley" girl was the woman who, for a period of a year, represented the company at all functions inside and outside the company. She participated in marketing campaigns for the company and appeared in photographs, advertising, and the company newsletter. In the late 1930s when the U.S. was recruiting soldiers, the "Hello Charley" girl's role also included greeting former employees in the military who visited the company on leave. The "Hello Charley" girl had a wholesome, girl next door image people adored.

Each year, after the tradition began, hundreds of women were nominated to be the year's "Hello Charley" girl. Elections were held in May and the "Hello Charley" girl and her court were crowned in June. The winner received a three piece luggage set and tags with the "Hello Charley" logo and the current "Hello Charley" Girl's photo.

*Ginny assisting at the Hobby Show.*

Of course, promotional items followed -- including auto stickers with the "Hello Charley" winner's photo, thus identifying Western Electric workers all over the world.[3] When the U.S. entered the war, additional promotional materials were created that included stickers with glue on the backside which could be affixed to military bags, shaving kits, and other items a soldier might carry with him. These stickers were sent to former employees with the company newsletter.

Ginny was nominated as a "Hello Charley" contestant in April of 1941. Her assistance at the April 21-25, 1941 Hobby Show, handing out flowers did not go unnoticed. 132 women were nominated and voting occurred throughout the company. The nominees were narrowed down to only five.

*The Hello Charley Court 1941. Left to right: Lucille Wilson, Kathleen Ryan, Virginia Scharer, Leona Redelsperger, Elinore Klobucar.*

On June 11, 1941, Ginny was elected the "Hello Charley" girl for 1941, after having been employed only six weeks. Ginny was so

Ginny's coronation photo and flowers.

fortunate to have been elected because it changed her life.

As "Hello Charley" girl, Ginny's duties included attending all company events, ribbon cutting ceremonies, various social functions, and representing Western Electric at events outside of the company. Ginny said for every event she attended, the company provided a different escort. Photographs were taken at every event. Afterward, articles were written for the company newsletter. Ginny's modeling skills and strong family values played a large role in her comportment during these events. As always, she was an exceptional company representative.

Ginny's war effort duties to support the troops required her to write letters to the former company employees serving in the military. She also greeted returning military personnel who stopped for a visit on leave.

Ginny's photo on The Microphone.

Over the course of her reign as "Hello Charley" girl, Ginny's photo traveled across the country. Employees both past and present sent her postcards from their travels. Soldiers, after seeing her sticker or visiting the plant, sent her letters. Ginny's photo appeared in the major Chicago newspapers at company events and in the company newsletter. Ginny's fame grew over the year. As a result, Ginny amassed a collection of letters and postcards in her scrapbook during her year as "Hello Charley" girl from soldiers and fans across the country.[4]

*Hello Charley!* 23

*Ginny and Lt. Barber posing for marketing photos which appeared (lower left) in The Microphone. Lower right, Ginny poses for another newsletter article.*

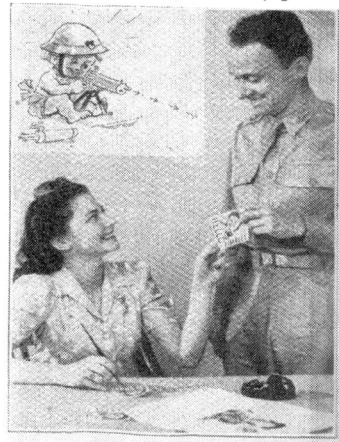

**GETS A PERSONAL "HELLO."** While on a visit to Hawthorne recently Lt. Barber, on military leave from our Equipment Engineering organization, was presented with a "Hello, Charley" sticker by Virginia Scharer (Dept. 942-1A), whose features are the feature of the 1941 vacation emblem.

AIR CORPS TECHNICAL SCHOOL
CHANUTE FIELD, ILLINOIS

June 17, 1941

Dear Virginia,

While reading the "Chicago Herald American" this evening our eyes were suddenly attracted to your picture. It is not often that we have the pleasure of viewing such an attractive girl.

We are Flying Cadets of the Class of November '41 at Chanute Field, where we are training to become Engineering Officers in the Air Corps.

It is too bad that you are not going to have a vacation, but we are in the same "boat." However, if permission is granted it is possible to obtain a three day leave beginning with the 4th of July. Since most of us live too far away from home, we will probably spend our time off in Chicago — it would be pleasant

*Letter to Virginia from Flying Air Corps Cadets in 1941.*

accident if we should meet.

Our day here is quite taken up with formations. We are up at 5:00 A.M., eat breakfast, class from 6:00 A.M. to 10:00 A.M., dinner at 10:00 A.M., class from 11:00 A.M. until 2:00 P.M., drill from 3:00 to 4:30 P.M., supper at 5:00 P.M., and "lights out" at 9:30 P.M. — what a day.

It would surely please us all if you could find time to write us about yourself, your work, and your activities since you have unanimously been chosen the "Queen of Flying Cadets."

Sincerely,

Flying Cadets:
George R. Walter
Thomas H. Bunt
Wm. H. Foster
Harlan O. Tibbitts
Erskine Roach
Marshall J. Cowan
Donald E. Flinn
Roy E. Fredricksen
Ralph E. Luther
John E. Kiningham
Hampton A. Hanley
Bill Blackburn

Eugene H. Duggan
Foster L. White
Thomas Nicholas Parker
Francis M. Blair
Howard F. Bell
Hans B Munger
Omer G. Potts
Malcolm C. Kaplan
Brady Jim
John H. Hoover
Leonard Rivers    E. C. Kraker
Wendell Phillips
Harold E. Reichenberg
William J. Chauvent

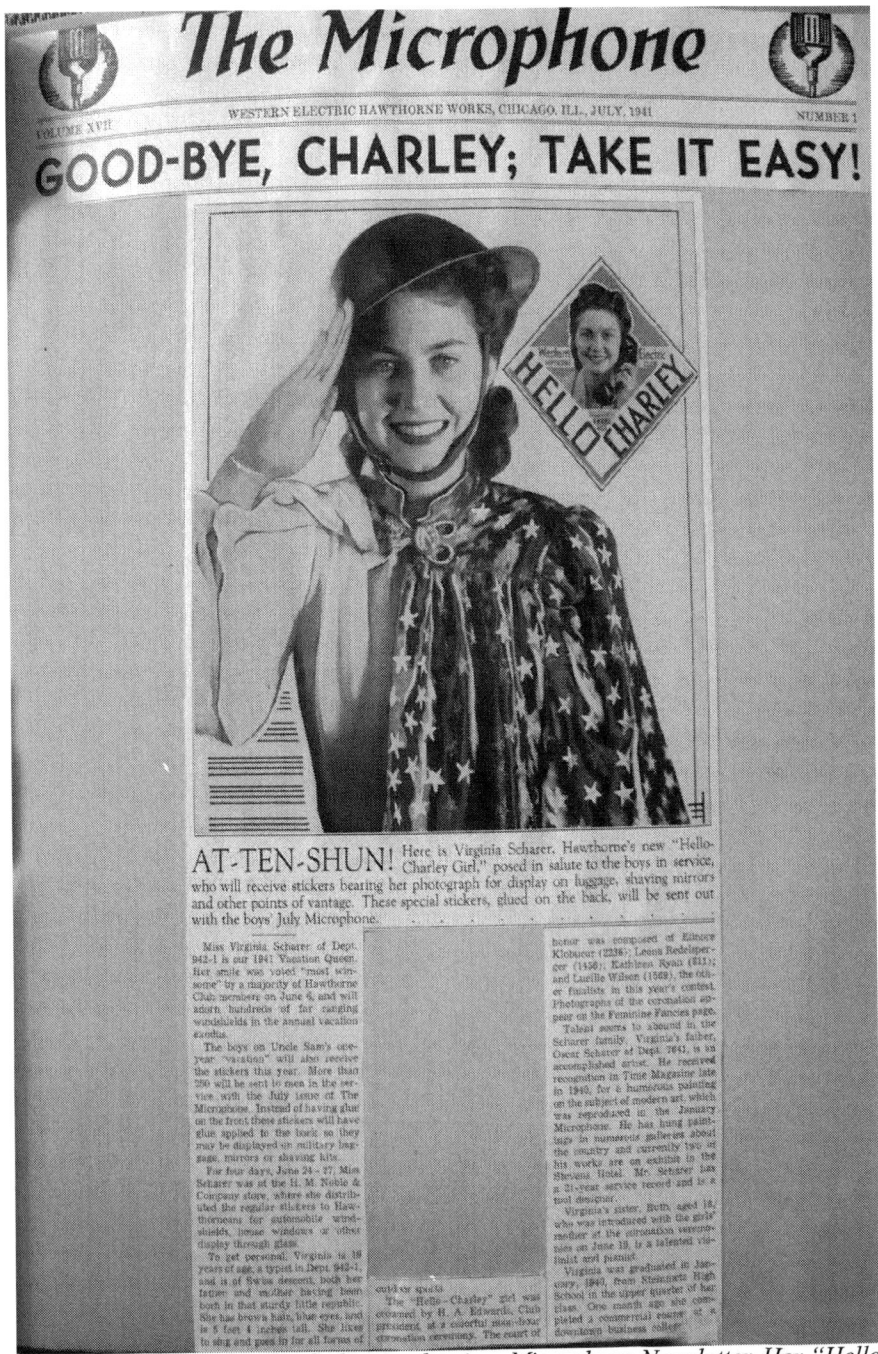

*Page from Ginny's scrapbook showing her in a Microphone Newsletter. Her "Hello Charley" stickers were sent to Hawthorne Works men in the military to adorn bags, shaving kits, and other personal items.*

During Ginny's year as the "Hello Charley" Girl, she was asked to star in the play This Thing Called Love. The Western Electric Theater company was floundering during 1941 and Ginny was suggested for the role because of her modeling experience. Ginny was not excited about this turn of events. She had no love for acting. Of course, her protective father supported her decision to not take the role, but it was her mother who convinced her to do it for the company. In the end, Ginny's performance as Ann Winters was a smash.

Ginny's year as the "Hello Charley" Girl made her job of order clerk bearable. The extra duties of a photo shoot, meeting a G.I or other event took her away from the tedious daily duties of an order clerk. She was able to enjoy her job, keep her father's protectiveness at bay, and play the perfect company girl.

*This Thing Called Love play photo and note from Ginny's scrapbook.*

## 28  Hello Charley!

# THE MICROPHONE
### WESTERN ELECTRIC HAWTHORNE WORKS CHICAGO · ILLINOIS

VOL. XVII    OCTOBER, 1941    NO. 4

THE
HAWTHORNE PLAYERS
(ASSOCIATED WITH HAWTHORNE CLUB)
present

"THIS THING CALLED LOVE"

A Farce in Three Acts

by

Edwin Burke

Directed by
Marjorie Flanagan

October 17 and 18, 1941
Lowell School

Produced by special arrangement with
Samuel French and Company
New York

HAWTHORNE CLUB
OFFICERS

President ..................... J. J. CONNERS
Vice President ................ R. C. BROWN
2nd Vice President ............ MISS H. C. SIRUTZ
Treasurer ..................... P. E. PETERMAN
Executive Secretary ........... E. L. F. HEINRICH

THE HAWTHORNE PLAYERS
wish to express their appreciation for the
stage furnishings supplied for them by the
LOWELL SCHOOL
and the
HAWTHORNE FURNITURE COMPANY
2214-16 S. 52nd Ave., Cicero
and to
THE SCHEFER FLORAL SHOP
4757 W. North Ave., Chicago
For Flowers Donated

**Players to Present Sparkling Comedy In October**

Casting for the Hawthorne Players' first presentation of the season, to be staged early in October, has been completed.

The play will be a light comedy by Edwin Booth, entitled "This Thing Called Love." The plot deals with the marital troubles of two young couples. One marriage is that of two persons in love, the other a marriage of two persons who do not believe in love.

The play will be under the direction of Marge Flanagan (Dept. 6131).

The cast follows:
Harry Bertrand — Bob Williams (3132); Florence Bertrand — Kinkla Pavlik (963); Ann Marvin — Viking Scuarra (242-1A); Danny Scuarra — Roy Veeglio (1431); Teddy Garrett — Lois Durkin (Installation); Fred Garrett — Bill Ramsay (319); Tice Collins — Tom Parker (313); Miss Alvarez — Alice Krampack (1165); Norma De Witt — Bea Kronpasch (607-2).

**"This Thing Called Love" Opens Players' Season**

"This Thing Called Love," presented at the Lowell School in Oak Park on October 17 and 18, was well received by the audience. The comedy was the first production this season by the Hawthorne Players. It was a well-built performance all the way through and a credit to the players and director.

Twenty-five consecutive rehearsals were necessary to whip the play into shape and these were supplemented by an equal amount of home study.

# 4

# Two Hearts Join

## Robert

Robert Ralph Brouk was born September 2, 1917, in Oak Park, Illinois. His father, Peter Brouk was a Bohemian immigrant, arriving in the United States January 5, 1900, at the age of 10.[5] His mother, Emily Novak, was born in Chicago to Bohemian immigrants. Peter and Emily had three children, Peter, born September 4, 1915, died April 1, 1922;[6] Robert; and Harold, born October 6, 1923, died December 23, 1983.[7] Harold joined the United States Army during World War II and was sent to Fort Warren, Wyoming, for training.[8] During World War II, Fort Warren served as a training base for U.S. Army Quartermaster Corps Soldiers.

Robert's father Peter was a sign painter, and took great pride in his community.[9] As a business owner, he was a member of the 22nd Street Business Men's Association in Cicero, where he served in the role of Secretary in 1931. The organization's goal was to revitalize and encourage growth of the businesses along 22nd Street in the villages of Cicero and Berwyn in the 1930s.[10]

As a child, Robert attended Woodrow Wilson grammar school. From 1931 until 1935, he attended J. Sterling Morton High School in Cicero, where he was active in campus clubs and sports. Robert participated in the Drum and Bugle Corps his freshman, sophomore, and junior years. Robert was a wrestler his Junior and Senior years. He also served as Vice-President of the Chemistry club his senior year; and played Intramural Sports his junior year.[11]

Robert graduated from Morton High School in Cicero, Illinois, in 1935.[12] After graduation, he attended Morton Junior College, in Cicero, from 1935 – 1937. While attending Morton during his freshman year, Robert participated in the Chemistry Club, Engineer's Club, and continued with his wrestling.

Fit in mind and fit in body, Robert was mentioned in a Morton wrestling article, in the Morton Collegian, because the college had the largest squad in years, and "Competition rife in the 135 lb. division with Robert Brouk…"[13] seems to speak to Robert's competitiveness and skill. The Morton Junior College Wrestling Team exceeded expectations in 1936 by winning against several four year colleges in the Chicago area.

Also during 1936, Robert was inducted on June 21st, as a Master Builder in the Cicero Chapter, No. 12, Order of the Builders.[14] The Order of Builders is still today, a part of the Masons, for boys ages 9 to 21, and its purpose is to teach the members the principles of democracy and ideals of Freemasonry, while participating in various social, athletic and civic projects. To be inducted, the boy must be a close relation to a current Masonic member. Robert's father, Peter Brouk, was a Mason in Cicero.

During Robert's sophomore year at Morton College, he again participated in the Chemistry Club and the wrestling team. The Wresting Team, in its second successive season, did not win as many matches as it had the year before. However, Robert was listed in the Pioneer Yearbook as one individual who consistently won the matches in which he competed.[15]

In the Morton Collegian Prophecy article about the sophomore graduating class, it was predicted that Robert would be, "Research expert for the We Chew Your Gum Co," which speaks to his probable sense of humor.[16] In the Pioneer Yearbook for 1937, it lists Robert Brouk as a Pre-Engineering Student who was, "Athletic, scholastic and sociable."[17] Robert graduated from Morton Junior College on June 13, 1937.

After graduating from Morton Junior College in 1935, Robert attended Lewis Institute of Technology. It was while attending Lewis in 1939, that Robert joined the Army Air Corps.[18] Robert graduated from the United States Army Air Corps Advanced Flying School on 30 August 1940, at Kelly Field, Texas. Upon graduation, Robert received his commission as a Second Lieutenant in the Army Air Corps Reserve.[19]

Later, while serving at Mitchel Field, Robert learned about the formation of the American Volunteer Group (AVG.) Mr. 'Skip' Adair of Central Aircraft Manufacturing Company (CAMCO) visited Mitchel Field to recruit pilots, mechanics, and armorers to join the AVG in China. The AVG was being formed by all volunteer pilots and ground crew under the leadership of Claire Lee Chennault.

In 1937, Chennault was a retired Captain of the U.S. Army Air Corps. He was working under the leadership of Madame Chaing Kai-shek between 1937 and 1941 to help China build an air force similar to the U.S. structured Army Air Corps. China was on the verge of war with Japan and needed assistance building a solid program and defense system.

After consulting for many months with the Chinese Air Force, Chennault handled the strategic planning of air raid systems, air fields, and pilot training. He flew many missions with the Chinese pilots against the Japanese and developed new combat strategies. He took this knowledge and proposed the formation of the AVG.[20]

In Chennault's mind, the purpose of the AVG was to defend China and Burma's main roads and supply routes from Japanese attack. He also wanted to attack Japanese staging areas and supply depots. To accomplish this, he needed a well-trained group of pilots and ground crew.

Without support from the U.S. Army Air Corps or U.S. Navy, who did not want to see volunteer American pilots in China, Chennault enlisted the aid of President Roosevelt. The president sent out

*Robert and Frank Losonsky.*

an unpublished executive order on April 15, 1941, encouraging pilots and ground crew to join the fight. These men would be honorably discharged from the U.S. Army Air Corps or Navy, to join the AVG and were hired by the Central Aircraft Manufacturing Company (CAMCO.) The president also authorized specific individuals to visit air fields to recruit pilots and ground crew. Mr. 'Skip' Adair of CAMCO visited Mitchel field in late April and early May 1941 where Robert was stationed. It was at here that Robert decided to join the AVG.

Why were the men of the AVG known as the Flying Tigers? Chennault explained it was simply because they painted the shark toothed design on the noses of their planes. This design was not original to them, but something they copied from a R.A.F. squadron that served in the Libyan Desert. Walt Disney's company then created insignia of the plane flying through a 'V' for Victory. The design and name caught on and people all across the country were calling these men the Flying Tigers.

The Flying Tigers were fighting against the Japanese before the U.S. was attacked at Pearl Harbor. The pilots became heroes to Americans after we entered the war for the work they were doing. Robert flew with the Flying Tigers until July 4, 1942 when the AVG was disbanded and the pilots and ground crew were re-inducted into the Army Air Corps to support the war effort.

## Robert Returns

During Ginny's reign as a "Hello Charley" girl, the U.S. joined the world war after the attack on Pearl Harbor by the Japanese. Ginny's duties at work remained almost the same, but she saw an increase in men leaving the company to join the military. The draft was also in effect which drew away more men to serve. Many of the company soldiers wrote to Ginny while they were in training. When they visited during leave, Ginny would welcome them at Western Electric.

Robert Brouk.

Winter of 1942 turned to spring and then summer. In July of 1942, one of the famous Flying Tigers of the American Volunteer Group (AVG), Robert Brouk, returned from service in China. After a brief visit with his parents, Robert began a tour of Chicagoland clubs, organizations, radio, and newspaper offices, and told the tale of his service with the Flying Tigers. Upon his arrival home, the local newspapers began running almost daily accounts of his comings and goings and life overseas while serving with the AVG.

After an interview with the Chicago Daily Tribune, it was written that "Robert recounts his experiences in a manner that is refreshingly modest and yet confident and alert. He is credited with knocking four Japanese planes out of the sky."[21]

Patriotic spirit was high and Robert became Cicero's "hometown hero" because of his engagement with the Japanese in the skies over China. The Berwyn Life newspaper began planning a parade and ceremony to honor Robert which would be held on August 2, 1942. The newspaper ran articles almost daily in the weeks before "Bob Brouk Day," praising the heroic efforts of Robert, the Flying Tigers, and other local men serving in the Armed Forces in the war.

As the interviews continued to keep Robert in the spotlight, the "Bob Brouk Day" planning committee continued their plans for the celebration. They decided Robert and his parents would travel by car at the head of the parade route as military and civic leaders followed. No floats were allowed in the parade, however all Cicero clubs and organizations were invited to participate in the parade and ceremony. Some of the groups that participated included: Boy Scouts, a group Robert was very involved in as a teen; Girl Scouts; Morton High School Band; Local American Legion Posts; Bohemian Sokols; Cicero Fire and Police Departments; Chinese Boy Scout Drum and Bugle Corps; Cicero Post American Legion Drum and Bugle Corps; and other musical and civic groups.

Amid all this planning, Robert continued to visit various local clubs, businesses, and organizations. He spoke about his experience as a Flying Tiger. It was on one of these visits, to the Western Electric Hawthorne Works Plant that Robert met his future wife, the "Hello Charley" girl, Virginia Scharer.

*Robert. Courtesy Hawthorne Works Museum.*

Robert and Ginny met at the homecoming ceremony Western Electric held for Robert on July 30, 1942. The event took place in the outdoor recreation area of the Plant where the employees caught a glimpse of the heroic ace. Ginny and another woman were asked to show him around the Plant and take him to lunch and make him feel at home.

Ginny described her first impressions of Robert. "He was so unassuming, kind and thoughtful. Therefore, I was flattered and excited when he said, 'Would you like to join me for a cup of chi after all this hullabaloo is over?' I joined him – we talked, and then dated and you know the rest."[22] The couple had a whirlwind romance. Ginny said, "As I look back now, it almost seems like God said, 'Hurry up, do things fast Robert. You only have a short time left on earth.'"[23]

*Robert (standing left). Seated, Peter and Harold Brouk.*

The month of July quickly ended, and "Bob Brouk Day" arrived on August 2. Thousands of local citizens lined the parade route in anticipation. The parade started at 2:00 p.m. and proceeded east on Cermak Road to the Western Electric Albright Memorial Field at Cermak Road and 50th Avenue. The parade line up was as follows: Division 1 – Military; Division II – Veterans; Division III – Sea Scouts, Boys Scouts, Girl Scouts; Division IV – Sign Painters Local Union No. 830; Division V – Civic; Division VI – Fraternal and Social.[24]

At 3:00 p.m., as initial vehicles in the parade lineup reached the Albright Memorial Field, a ceremony opened with the "Star Spangled Banner" sung by a schoolmate of Robert's, Keith Smejkal. The anthem was followed by a prayer given by Bob's former chaplain in China, Reverend Paul Frillman. The prayer was followed by a speech by Mr. David Levinger, the Vice-President of Western Electric Hawthorne Works. Major Lloyd M. Showalter of the U.S. Army Air Corps followed and finally after many other speakers, Robert was introduced and interviewed. After Robert's speech, his parents were introduced before Robert presented Gold Stars to the families of Cicero's three known World War II Service fatalities. Following the presentation, a "parade in the sky" was held. Planes were flown from the Army Air Corps units, the Illinois Air Militia and the Civil Aeronautics Air Patrol.[25]

*Robert in Bob Brouk Day Parade.*

Thousands of people lined Cermak Road and filled Albright Memorial Field for "Bob Brouk Day." It was a sight to behold. Everyone wanted to see the famous Flying Tiger. During Robert's speech on a podium at the field, Ginny and Robert's parents stood near the front to witness this piece of history. The Flying Tiger stood proud in his uniform, a symbol of hope for the country. It was a day no one would ever forget.

Summer drew to a close, fall arrived, and with it a great change. Robert and Ginny continued to date, their hearts linked together as Robert continued visiting local organizations to speak. It was a time of war and the Army needed him. Robert rejoined the Army Air Corps and The Berwyn Life reported on October 12, 1942, that Robert was on his way to Washington, D.C., "in anticipation of orders which probably will transfer him to Orlando, Fla., as a flying instructor."[26] The report was correct, Robert was promoted to the rank of Captain, and in October he was stationed in Orlando, Florida, at the newly formed Army Air Forces School of Applied Tactics (AAF-SAT).[27][28] Robert was assigned to the 81st Pursuit Squadron, 50th Fighter Group, 10th Fighter Squadron. Charles Bond, a fellow Flying Tiger from the 1st Squadron, served as the 81st Pursuit Squadron's Commander during that time.

Robert and Ginny continued to date in the early fall and their bond and love for each other grew. In October, Robert reported for duty in Orlando, Florida where he was stationed to train pilots, Virginia remained in Chicago with her family.

During World War II, people learned to live more fully in the moment and love with their whole hearts. You never knew what the next day would bring. Not wanting to be apart because the two were so in love, Robert proposed to Ginny on October 30, 1942, over the phone. He sent his parents a telegram announcing his proposal. Ginny spoke to her father about the proposal and he said, "Do you love him?" and after she answered yes, he said "All right, but remember it will be a permanent life style change."[29] Truer words were never spoken.

Life moved quickly after Robert's proposal. With Robert in Orlando on duty until shortly before their wedding, it was up to Virginia to plan the wedding, obtain the marriage license, and prepare to move to Florida. The Daily Times, Chicago, reported on November 25, "She went down to the city hall yesterday and obtained a marriage license for herself and her fiancé, Capt. Robert Brouk…"[30] The two were to be married three days later on November 28, 1942 at 8:00 p.m. at the First Congregational Church in Oak Park. Despite the time crunch, Virginia was able to put together a beautiful wedding party.

After the wedding, Robert and Virginia drove to Orlando and created a home at 1209 E. Kaley. Ginny wrote about her first two weeks in the house in her memoir. She wrote about unpacking and putting their new home together. They were young and in love with their whole lives ahead of them.

*Robert and Ginny's wedding photo.*

# 5
# The Final Flight

On December 19, 1942, Ginny woke up ecstatic because Robert was due home that morning. He had been training pilots in Kissimmee, Florida for several days and Ginny missed him. After all, they were still newlyweds. Feeling breathless with excitement, Ginny arrived at the airfield and sat on the hood of her car near the base hangar. She watched as the planes appeared on the horizon. The anticipation of his return grew as she contemplated the rest of the day with her husband. Finally he was home!

Nearing his destination at the Orlando Air Base, Robert was the lead plane in a formation of six planes. What a magnificent sight! The planes rose and dove in formation as they practiced maneuvers. Ginny watched the squadron practice strafing runs over the field. Her heart raced as she watched the action unfold.

The ships in Robert's formation, along with other formations, simulated a strafing of the Orlando airfield. As the strafing simulation was being attempted, what Ginny did not know was First Lieutenant Sidney O. Kane's plane, flying in the number two position, flew too close to Robert's plane as Robert began to pull up and turn left.

What happened next was inconceivable. As the planes zoomed across the sky, soared to great heights and dove toward the earth, a plane suddenly dropped from the sky. Flying just a few hundred feet off the ground, Lt. Kane's wing tip touched Robert's right wing tip. This small action caused Robert's plane to immediately flip upside down, crash, and explode in a giant fireball. What remained of his plane was almost unrecognizable as aircraft. As the fireball erupted Ginny quietly watched, not quite sure what has just happened. Who was the pilot?

Witnesses reported Lt. Kane's plane flew on a short distance, gained some altitude and then turned and crashed into a field. He did not survive.

"I watched the planes pass overhead, then turn and prepare for a landing when all of a sudden two planes collided in mid-air and fell to the ground. Shocked, I sat there in silence and just stared until some people came and informed me that one of the planes was Bob's." Ginny recalled.[31]

In shock and numb, Ginny was unable to believe the man she fell in love with and married three weeks ago was gone. A life ended in that moment and their plans, hopes, and dreams vanished in a fireball.

Ginny was in such shock, her memories of the events after the crash were hazy. It was too much for a 20 year old new bride to process. Moments before the crash she was excitedly anticipating her new husband's return and a day together. But it was not to be.

Her blood pressure soared and she was put in bed and packed in ice to bring the pressure down. The next thing Ginny remembered was she phoned her in-laws to tell them Robert had died. Still in shock, she did as instructed by the military captain assigned to escort her home, packed a bag and departed for the train station.

Things happened quickly and an Army Captain escorted Ginny home to Chicago by train with Bob's remains. Three days she rode the train with almost no conversation. Was the Army Captain just as shook up as she was about Bob's death? Or did he just not know what to say?

Upon arrival in Chicago, the Army Captain quietly deposited Ginny at the door of her parent's home and quickly departed. The family prepared for Robert's funeral and grieved in the privacy of their home.

The wake and funeral were more than Ginny could bear. She was only 20, a new bride, and now widow, with her entire life ahead of her. Thousands of people arrived at the wake to pay their respects. The crowd pushed and pulled on all sides of the family which made it difficult to breathe or move. Ginny was unable to grieve as she wanted, therefore she choose to remain strong and composed. The grieving came later, at home, alone with the support of her family. Ginny drew on her experience in public relations from her "Hello Charley" days. She knew how to remain composed and do and say the correct thing.

After the wake, the multitude of flowers sent for the wake was loaded into cars as the family prepared to leave the funeral home. The journey to the cemetery was a short drive from the funeral home but it felt never ending. Thousands came out to witness the procession and pay their respects and mourn for Cicero's Hometown Hero, the famous Flying Tiger, Robert Brouk.

After the family arrived at the cemetery, Ginny was seated with Robert's parents and hers in the front row at the gravesite. She looked down in front of her and saw an open hole waiting to consume her husband's casket which sat nearby in preparation for burial. Reverend Coe, the man who married them three short weeks ago gave a beautiful service, or so she was told. This was a service of which Ginny remembered very little. Still numb and in shock, she did as she was told and remained strong enough to get through the horrible ordeal.

At the end of the service, sitting by the grave, Ginny watched as the servicemen removed the flag from the casket. They solemnly and precisely folded the flag and presented it to her as Taps was mournfully played. The notes drifted through the air carrying pieces of Robert and Ginny's brief life together. At the conclusion of the final somber note, very gently and quietly, Robert's casket was lowered into the ground.

As this happened, Ginny felt her heart beating quickly into a million pieces in her chest. Her nerves shattered as the world closed in on her in the great open space of the cemetery. Just as grief was about to overtake her, it became more than she could handle, quietly, she fell to the ground and fainted.

Ginny found herself at home with her family after the service and wondered how she would handle the grief. This was too much for one person to handle. She thought herself, 'I'm so young and still a newlywed.' She questioned if the pain and grief would ever subside.

*****

Robert's short life affected many people, and he was honored in numerous ways. After Robert's death, Virginia received a letter from the War Department sending their condolences on his tragic accident.

In early March of 1943, Madame Chiang Kai-Shek visited Chicago. Many concerts and events were held in her honor during the weeks she visited the city. Virginia received an invitation to attend a reception and tea on March 12, 1943, at the Palmer House in Chicago. Virginia remembered Madame Chiang Kai-Shek as a very cultured and charming woman who remembered Robert and his 3rd Squadron of the Flying Tigers.[32]

*Ginny meets Madame Chiang Kai-Shek.*

The Hawthorne Works Newsletter, The Microphone, featured Virginia in an article about her meeting with Madame Chiang Kai-Shek and explained the large scarf she wore was in appreciation of Robert's service in China. The small scarf-like item on the right side of the photo is a cloth which was sewn on the back of all of the Flying Tiger's Uniforms to ensure that if they were shot down, the Chinese people would assist the pilots.[33]

Shortly after Robert's death, Virginia returned to work at the Hawthorne Works Plant. She realized there comes a time when no one will pull you up out of the darkness and despair of such a great loss but yourself. It was up to her alone to figure out how to heal and move forward. She still had the rest of her life to live.

After much deliberation, Ginny decided to take up Robert's fight and join the Women's Army Auxiliary Corps (WAACs). This was a way to serve the country in a time of war, travel the world to places Robert had served (she hoped,) and contribute to the war effort. Plans for the rest of Ginny's life, in that moment, were set in motion.

# 6
# The Decision to Join the Fight

The culture and mindset at the time of World War II was primarily that women stayed home. They were the homemakers, mothers, wives, and daughters, whose job it was to run the house. This meant to cook, clean, do the laundry, raise the children, run errands, and take care of their fathers or husbands. Women were supposed to be feminine and nurturing. A college education was unheard of in many families because the role of women was that of a housewife. Women in general were not viewed as warriors or capable of taking up the fight. War was a deadly place, a place for men not women.

When women began enlisting in the service, whether it was in the Army (WAACs and later WACs), Navy (WAVES), Army Air Corps (WASPs), Coast Guard (SPARs), Women Marine recruits, Red Cross or USO workers, or Nurses, there was pushback in some families. Attitudes such as 'what can women possibly do to help the war effort?' 'Scrubbing bathrooms for the Navy is not helping win the war.' And, 'A woman's place is in the home,' were common thoughts and feelings.

Women had to find the strength within themselves to defy the usual role delegated to them, to join the fight. Once they found that strength, nothing could stop them from doing their part.

In talking to women who served, they may tell you they felt they did not do much or enough to win the war. The men were the ones on the front lines fighting and giving their lives. They were the heroes. They were the important ones in the war effort. Women were simply not. The pushback and attitude from families contributed to the feeling of women who served in World War II that they didn't do anything or contribute as much as a man. This is untrue. Women contributed much to the war effort whether they served in the Armed Forces or on the home front.

On the home front, women grew Victory gardens and helped collected recyclable materials for the war effort. They ran the home, raised the children, and often got jobs outside the home while their husbands were fighting. They bonded more closely with family and neighbors to help each other get through that terrible time. They worked in war factories building airplanes and ordnance. They filled jobs the men left behind when they went off to fight.

In the Armed Forces, women replaced men who could be sent off to fight. They took over the clerical jobs, weather forecasting, parachute rigging, medical, and mechanical jobs, just to name a few. Some of these women had some college education or training behind them before taking on these more technical positions. The majority did not but they were sent to training schools to learn. This training provided more options after the war should they decide marriage and family was not for them.

What were these women doing to benefit future generations of women? They laid the foundation for women to have the opportunity to serve in the military. The option to work outside the home in jobs which were more than the teaching and clerical jobs women typically held during the 1940s. More women began going to college and forgoing marriage because they learned they could be more and do more. Marriage was not the only option.

These women gave future generations the inspiration and power to dream big and do the impossible. They gave future generations the option of a richer life with fewer restrictions on what was allowed in the work place. No longer was marriage the only life open to American women. An entire new world awaited the 1940s woman and her descendants.

## Women's Army Auxiliary Corps (WAAC) History

A woman serving in the military arena was not new to World War II. In World War I, nurses filled the ranks and served. By World War II it became evident women were needed to help fill jobs men held so they could be released for duty. Men were needed for the infantry and other areas to help win the war. Women were not allowed to take up arms but could fill other necessary positions anywhere in the world they were needed. They were given military rank, uniforms, and training. They had to abide by the fifth General Order, "I will not quit my post until properly relieved."[34]

The Women's Army Auxiliary Corps (WAAC) was formed on May 14, 1942 when Congress passed a bill to create a new section of the Army led by Oveta Culp Hobby. The original plan was to recruit 150,000 women into service but Congress adopted a limit of 25,000. This limit was met very quickly and the goal was raised to the original 150,000 by the end of 1942.[35] WAACs had to be between the ages of 21 and 45 with no dependents. They were to be at least 5' tall and weigh 100 pounds.

Why would a woman consider joining the WAAC? There were many reasons such as wanting to serve their country; honor a male family member who was fighting or who had died; a desire to end the war sooner; and the ability to free up a job so a man could be sent to fight.[36] WAACs received medical and dental benefits, furlough, free mail, and use of the Army Exchange as part of their service.[37]

WAAC enlisted personnel were sent to training camp, the first of which was established at Fort Des Moines, Iowa. Training was similar to that of an Army man regarding classroom training, physical training, and close order drills. The women however were not trained in the use of guns and artillery. The women were required to have short, neat haircuts which were above the collar. They could wear subtle make-up and nail polish. Uniforms had to be neat and pressed and the only allowable jewelry was watches, signet rings and wedding rings.[38]

From basic training, graduates were put into the Army Air Forces (AAF,) Army Ground Forces (AGF,) or Army Service Forces (ASF) to serve. Contingents of WAACs were formed with roughly 150 women. The makeup of a unit was three commissioned officers, 22 noncommissioned officers and the rest enlisted personnel. Each contingent was similar yet this standard number as not always required, depending on what the Army requested.

The typical jobs WAACs encountered were office jobs. Later in the war, the women were moved into additional areas where men could be released from jobs as weather observers, engineers, control tower operators, photographers, and broadcasters.

By 1943, the WAAC was getting a bad reputation and enlistment numbers were declining. Men serving in the armed forces felt a woman's place was in the home, not in the Army. Rumors were spreading through the men's ranks that the WAACs were prostitutes and supposed to be showing the fighting men a good time. Rumors of pregnancy spread. Men fighting wanted their worlds at home to remain the same. It is what kept them going through the hard times. If women were joining the ranks, even in non-combat jobs, their worlds were changing. They didn't like this. Letters were written home to sisters, daughters, and wives of men serving threatening disinheritance or divorce if their wives or sisters or daughters joined the WAAC.[39]

It didn't matter if the rumors were unfounded or that the majority of fighting men had never encountered a WAAC. The fact is, times were different then and women had certain roles they played. The fact is women were beginning to step out of traditional roles to support the war effort and in the process were becoming more independent, this was not a happy thought for many men.[40]

Also in 1943, the Army wanted to see the WAAC become part of the Army, working with it, not alongside it. On July 3, 1943, a bill was passed and the WAAC was dissolved. Women were given the option to join the Women's Army Corp (WAC) and enjoy the benefits and protection of all those serving in the Army. It was not long after this change that WACs began going overseas to combat areas such as North Africa, Mediterranean, Europe, the Southwest Pacific, China, India, Burma, and the Middle East.

# 7
# Ginny's WAAC Experience

*Ginny inducted into the Women's Army Auxiliary Corps.*

WAAC inductees had to be at least 21 years old, which meant Virginia had to wait until her 21st birthday to be inducted. On her 21st birthday, April 5, 1943, while wearing Robert's insignia in memory of him, Virginia was sworn into the WAAC. She requested service with the Air Force in the hopes of seeing parts of Burma where Robert flew.[41] Unfortunately, her request was denied.

What Ginny did not realize until much later, is that the WAAC was going to use her notoriety as a "Hello Charley" girl and her status as the widow of Flying Tiger Robert Brouk to aid their recruiting campaign. Newspapers had continually reported on Virginia as the widow of the Flying Tiger. As The Tiger's Widow, Virginia would gain more sympathy from other women considering joining the WAAC.

The first occurrence of this took place on April 8, just days after her birthday, when Ginny was asked to speak on WLS radio in Chicago. Her topic was the place of women in World War II. With no time to prepare, Ginny was on the radio beginning a public relations career for the WAACs. Two days later she spoke on radio station WENR in a program titled, "A Woman's War."[42]

Virginia received Special Orders No. 107 on May 4, 1943, to report for duty. The orders stated in part, the following.

> *By direction of the Secretary of War, each of the following named Enrolled Auxiliaries, WAAC, is ordered to active duty effective May 9, 1943, and time as will enable her to arrive thereat 7:30 P.M. May 10, 1943, reporting to the Officer in Charge at the rendezvous point, Armed Forces Induction station, 7th Floor, 166 w. Van Buren St., Chicago, Ill., for temporary duty, and will, when ordered, proceed to FT. OGLETHORP, GEORGIA, reporting to the Commanding Officer, Third WAAC Training Center, Ft. Oglethorpe, Georgia, May 11, 1943, for further disposition.*[43]

The *Chicago Times* on May 15, 1943, reported that Virginia was the 13,000 WAAC to be processed at Fort Oglethorpe and she was the widow of Flying Tiger Robert Brouk.[44] Again, the WAAC was using her notoriety for recruiting. This theme, Virginia as the widow, would play out in multiple newspaper articles for months into her WAAC and WAC career.

Virginia attended basic training at Fort Oglethorpe, Georgia. Each WAAC was issued everything they needed to survive in the Women's Army Corps. Equipment included duffle bags to hold all the gear, panties, slips, blouses, skirts, rayon hose, cotton hose, bras, girdles, summer and winter pajamas, low heeled shoes, a Hobby hat (named after Oveta Culp Hobby the Director), and jackets and coats.[45] WAACs were also subjected to physicals, gynecological exams, and the usual retinue of immunizations given in the Army.

During basic training Ginny was up by 5:30 a.m. to dress, make her bed, prepare for the day and attend reveille at 6:00 a.m. Her day was spent in training classes until 5:00 p.m. with a break for lunch. Classes included first aid, military customs and organization, watching films about venereal disease and the importance of keeping quiet, "Loose lips sink ships," and physical fitness. Her favorite part of basic training was marching and the close order drills, while her least favorite part was Kitchen Police (K.P.)[46] After dinner, WAACs were required to attend sessions about the care of their uniform and shoes, and attend to any personal needs such as bathing, laundry, and letter writing.

*WAAC Training Center at Fort Oglethorpe, GA.*

Upon completion of basic training, Ginny received Special Order Number 191 on July 22, 1943, which assigned her to the 9th Service Command at Fort Douglas, Utah. The Special Order read as follows.

> *The following named auxiliaries, WAAC, (SSN 936) are held from assignment and duty Co 1, 22nd Training Regiment this station, and are assigned permanent status at Headquarters, 9th Service Command, Fort Doulas, Utah, for duty as indicated, and will proceed to new station without delay, reporting upon arrival to the CO thereof for assignment and duty.*
>
> *This movement will be by rail. TO will furnish necessary Travel. IGF rations in kind, meal tickets for twelve (12) meals*

*will be furnished each auxiliary under provisions of Paragraph 2, AR 30-2215.*

*(The movement to the Staging Area, this station, will be between breakfast and dinner on Friday, 23 July 1943.)*[47]

At Fort Douglas, her jobs were to recruit girls, speak on her radio program, "A Woman's War," and be a Close Order Drill Sergeant.[48] As part of her duties, Ginny was required to dress in the WAAC uniform and pajamas and parade on stage at the movies during intermission in an attempt to recruit. Her days as a model prior to being a "Hello Charley" girl were coming in handy again in her role as WAAC model. In the 1940s movies were not double features. The first movie played then there was an intermission during which news reels would play and announcements would be made. During intermission, Ginny would give a short speech and attempt to recruit new WAACs. After the intermission another movie played.

In Salt Lake City, Utah, Ginny lived with four other WAACs at Hotel Utah. These women recruited others, primarily Mormons, for the WAAC at headquarters. The recruiters traveled to nearby areas in order to recruit. Much of the recruiting was done in person rather than by telephone. Many families wanted one on one discussions with a current WAAC about the duties and responsibilities. Some interviews were conducted in the homes of the potential recruits.

Not only did Ginny recruit in person, but she also participated in weekly radio programs during the time served in Utah. While many of these original transcripts no longer exist, Ginny still had three in her possession. The first program transcript she had was called, "This Could Be My Job."[49]

Top: Ginny after Basic Training at Fort Oglethorpe.

Bottom: WAACs. Ginny 2nd from left.

Press Release
Sub-Station Recruiting District, Provo, Utah

"This Could Be My Job"

Cpl. Virginia Brouk

Remember way back, years and years ago? You were just a little baby; mother's precious little bundle of joy. As the days, months, and years passed you grew up into a lovely young lady. All these past years you went to school; you have become educated, and have learned right from wrong. Whenever you heard of something new you asked questions. Therefore, when the Women's Army Corps (WAC's) first organized as an Auxiliary, you wanted to know all about it.

You learned the Women's Army Corps was an organization formed to release a man for combat duty; by having a girl replace this soldier for the front lines; a father could remain home with his children. Then too, the experience of being in the corps would be of great value later on in civilian life.

When you heard about the corps you thought it was a wonderful organization. But you wanted to know more about the different types of jobs the girls could do. To date you have probably not learned about all of them. Therefore, we will go through as many as we possibly can, taking one special job each week.

After reading this series of Army jobs, and how they work, you will have added another "answer" to your many questions.

Under the Technical and Professional heading we have: Medical, Personnel, Public Relations, Instruction and Training, Physical Sciences and Mathematics, Photography, Languages, Drafting, Weather, and Miscellaneous.

Each one of these occupations takes years of schooling and a great deal of experience before one can accomplish the tasks put before him.

Our first topic for this week will be connected with the Medical Field. This field alone consists of Dental technician, flight surgeon's assistant, hospital orderly (WAC's Nurse's Aide), Medical Laboratory Technician, medical Technician, Pharmacists, Sanitary Technician, Surgical Technician, and X-Ray Technician.

The WAC technicians do blood chemistry and cultures. They assist in taking X-Rays, and develop X-Ray film. In hospital jobs the WAC's assist in preparing antitoxins and vaccines, make up reports of hospital departments, and supervise the care of equipment.

If a woman is interested in this kind of work in the WAC she may attend the Enlisted Technician's School of eight weeks. This course is for medical and Surgical Technicians. Medical Technicians are taught anatomy and physiology, and emergency medical treatment. Surgical Technicians are trained in similar subjects, but their work is also done in surgical wards.

Dental, laboratory and X-Ray Technicians school takes twelve weeks to complete. In these courses WACs are trained in Army hospital procedure. Dental technicians learn dental anatomy, the keeping of dental records, dental hygiene, and X-Ray procedures.

Laboratory technicians learn hematology, chemistry, serology, and pathology. They are trained to do gastric analysis, urinalyses, and blood chemistry.

X-Ray Technicians learn how to take and develop X-Rays, Fluoroscopy, and the localization of foreign bodies.

When a WAC has completed her schooling and has proven her worth, she replaces a soldier for combat duty. What she has learned will probably follow her throughout her entire life.

After Virginia had served a few months in the WAAC, Congress passed a bill on September 1, 1943, dissolving the WAAC. In its place was the Women's Army Corp (WAC). Virginia joined the WAC and her rank was reduced again to Private.[51] It was at this time she began working for Major Oliver Shaffer with the 9th Service Command at 179 Motor Avenue in Salt Lake City. Once the change occurred, she and other WACs began changing the recruiting posters from Women's Army Auxiliary Corps to Women's Army Corps.

*Ginny and Major Oliver Shaffer.*

Virginia wrote a press release announcing the change after the bill was passed. It reads as follows.[51]

Press Release
Utah Recruiting District Headquarters
179 Motor Avenue, Salt Lake City, Utah

On September 1, 1943, the Women's Army Corps officially came into being as an integral part of the United States Army, superseding the Women's Army Auxiliary Corps.

This changeover from the "WAAC to the WAC marks an important milestone for the women who are serving in this war," believes Captain Mary Lois House, Utah district WAC recruiting officer.

"The Act creating the WAC is recognition of the accomplishments of the 65,000 women who already have volunteered," Captain House declared. "In the space of one year, these women have served their country earnestly and unselfishly in the WAAC. They have performed ably and well. The measure of their performance has been the demand for more and more WACs to fill over increasing numbers and types of jobs," she declared.

"Beginning September 1, all women who are accepted for enlistment will be sworn into the Women's Army Corps," Captain House said. A present, there is a great demand for more women from this area in the WAC to fill the positions already open for them in the Army.

"Women who wish to serve their country can find no better or more direct way than in the WAC," Captain House said.

Under provisions of the bill making the WAC an actual part of the Army, the age limits have been changed so that women between the ages of 20 and 50, inclusive, who meet other requirements may now enlist.

The size of the Corps is now unrestricted, whereas before this important change it was limited to 150,000. Various branches of the Army have made requests for some 500,000.

Another change made by the legislation is WAC officers may take on operational duties, whereas only command and administrative duties were allowed under the WAAC.

Under the new law, a WAC is eligible for the same benefits, privileges and pensions as male members of the Army with the exception that she is not covered by the soldier's allotment act.

The free mail privilege is to be extended to the Corps under the new law as well, according to Captain House.

*Ginny and a fellow WAC changing the WAAC signs.*

## STRTICTLY G.I.

Virginia wrote and presented another undated radio broadcast through the radio program STRICTLY G.I. which is as follows.[52]

>WAC Detachment
>Sub-station Utah Recruiting Section
>Provo, Utah
>
>Radio Broadcast ....................Provo, Utah.

Music (10 seconds) fades out as announcer speaks.....

ANNC: Good afternoon, ladies and gentlemen of Provo. We are about to present the first of the weekly WAC program called "STRICTLY G.I.", to be presented each week over this same station, the same time. This program is to inform you about the Women's Army Corps, and their work. You know the WAC has a military mission. It is composed of women serving with our soldiers, filling non-combatant Army jobs and releasing men to the battle front. Thousands more patriotic American women are urgently needed to fill these Army jobs, and speed the day of victory. Go to your nearest Army recruiting station, 209 Post Office Bldg, in Provo. And now to introduce to you our two members of the Women's Army Corps....the WAC's. We have with us in the studio this afternoon, Lt. Eleanor McAuliffe, and Cpl. Virginia Brouk (broke). Cpl. Brouk will you take over now?

BROUK: I most certainly will Mr…….. and thank you. Ladies and gentlemen…… As I speak to you this afternoon, over 65,000 American Women are replacing men in the army ----- releasing those men for combat duty. But let's look back a bit ---- to the facts behind it ---- let's look back on December 7th, 1941 ----- You might have been coming from church ----- just walking along any street in America. There are many streets alike, you know, with bare adolescent trees sketched against the sky ----- the gray skies of America in December. And you might have thought how graceful the silver body was against the sky --- and you might have drawn your kid gloves on and held your bus fare in the palm of your right hand ---- and then you might have heard. Someone might have tapped you on the shoulder ---- some stranger, some other American ---- and someone might have said to you: "Did you hear the news?" and you might have looked at that strange face and seen disaster there. And then there were other words ---- Pearl Harbor ---- Japan ---- attacked ---- WAR ---- and the palm of your fist closed on the coin you held

---- and you forgot about taking the bus ---- and you walked through the streets through America's streets anywhere, any town in America, and you walked as any American woman walked that day ---- to the beat of one word: WAR ---- WAR ---- WAR ---- That was the day American women asked ---- no ---- demanded their right to contribute vitally to victory. Even more urgent than the demands was the military necessity for women to do the necessary jobs behind the lines, to release men for actual fighting --- to strike back for December 7th ---- to avenge Pearl Harbor. But there are other battles ---- other theatres of the disease that is war. There's North Africa and the Solomons, ---- there's Russia and Bataan ---- and the desperate need for men. That is why the Women's Army Corps is so very important. The WAC's release these desperately needed men for combat duty. Women of America ---- Your country is calling for help ---- Back her up now, and help those boys at the fighting front. We will now hear a recording of .........

BROUK: Lt. McAuliffe, that music just put me in the mood to ask you some questions.

MC: Why yes, Cpl. Brouk go right ahead.

BROUK: Did you read the article "I Learned About Women From Them?" Written by Colonel Frank U. McCoskrie, Commandant of the Women's Army Corps training center at Fort Des Moines, Iowa?

MC: Yes I did Virginia, and there were so many good points in it, that, I believe, it would be nice if we could bring out some parts to our radio listeners. For instance, in one of his paragraphs he writes, "Women join the WAC for three reasons ---- patriotism, adventure, and curiosity. In that order. And the first, by far, is patriotism.

BROUK: Yes, I remember reading that too, and I do

believe he is correct. Most of the girls enlisting in the corps have a great deal of love for their country, and want to see her come out on top.

MC: That is the way we feel about Utah and the All-States WAC recruiting campaign. We want Utah to be ahead of every other state by having the largest contingents, and of course, the best contingents to arrive at the basic training centers.

BROUK: What appeals to me most of all is the fact that the girls may go through their basic training together with their girlfriends from the same state. I think you can have so much fun together.

MC: Yes, I quite agree with you Virginia. And did you know Col. McCoskrie, also states that WAC's take such pride in their discipline that you can tell them to do almost anything and they'll obey unflinchingly

BROUK: And too, Lt. McAuliffe, in this article it says that WAC's like to salute, and consider it an honor to do so. ---- The funniest thing I ever heard about this saluting situation was when a rookie walked between two officers, and became confused as to which one she should salute; so she saluted with both hands.

And now for another recording of ................

BROUK: That was a lovely piece. Lt. McAuliffe, I believe we will have time enough to hear about some of the Army jobs these girls can take over. Would you mind telling them about some of the jobs?

MC: Well, you girls know that we women take the non-combatant jobs, and even an unskilled person; after attending specialist schools may become skilled in some kind of work which will no doubt, be beneficial to the girl after the war is won ---- Since the corps is still growing, there are a great many opportunities for women in all fields. That noiseless Underwood, that Remington Rand, or your Royal Typewriter spells victory each time you hit a key for Uncle Sam. Bookkeepers, clerks, and secretaries help bring the war to an end sooner. If you are mechanically inclined you would like to drive the Japs away in a Jeep. By transporting material or chauffeuring cars another man may go to the fighting front. They say an Army moves on its stomach. Cooks and bakers school can make anyone domestically inclined. There are opportunities in the fields of draftsmanship, dental assistants, Cadres, Photographers, and even Parachute riggers. Then too, there are openings for telephone operators. It would be impossible for me to cover all the jobs a WAC can do, in the short time allowed now. However, you can rest assured there are plenty of jobs open in any field.

BROUK: Yes, Lt. McAuliffe, and if the women will just pay us a visit in Room 209, in the Post Office Building, we will be only too glad to speak with them, and answer any questions they may have. We are open from 8:00 A.M. to 5:00 P.M. for your convenience, and our telephone is 667.

ANNC: You have just been listening to STRICTLY G.I. the weekly WAC program presented each week over this same station the same time.

MC: Remember, you have a date at 209 Post Office Building. We'll be waiting.

BROUK: Please do not fail the fighting men. Good afternoon, friends.

Virginia stayed in touch with her friends at Western Electric while she served in the WAC. The Microphone, Western Electric's newsletter printed pieces of her letters to the company. In one dated,

September 2, 1943, she discussed the job she did in the WAC in Utah and what Army life was like.[53]

### PVT. VIRGINIA S. BROUK, WAC

Typist, Dept. 942. Excerpts from her letter of Sept. 2 to her department.

"At the present time I am working for the Public Relations Section in Salt Lake City and find the work very fascinating indeed. My day's work consists of interviewing WAC recruits and Aviation Cadets. I then write stories and articles for our three newspapers, "The Salt Lake Tribune," "The Desert," and "The Telegram." Once a week I speak over the radio, and put in that WAC plug. My afternoons are usually spent by writing speeches which we give at the churches, theaters, private parties, etc. I was always under the impression that I could talk (at least in Dept. 942) and now I am thoroughly convinced.

Army life is somewhat similar to civilian life when living in the city away from a camp. We do not have reveille, inspection or bed check. Instead, we have maid service – a private phone and the point system ration problem. With my appetite as it is, and my income as it is too, I find it rather difficult to make ends meet. But the fact that we are residing at the best hotel in the city compensates my other disappointments.

How long will I remain here I do not know. In this Army, one is never certain of anything, so we just live out of our barracks bag and wait for the word "move," but I love it.

Each and every one of us has great hopes of returning to our friends eventually, and I'll venture to say I have found the nicest friends of all when I walked through Gate 1 for the first time. You can not possibly imagine how many times I have thought of you and how many times I have thanked you for helping me.

Ginny included a piece of something she wrote and spoke of in her memoir. It reads as follows.[54]

> WAC Detachment
> Utah Recruiting District Headquarters
> 179 Motor Avenue, Salt Lake City, Utah
>
> RADIO BROADCAST:
> Saturday, September 25, 1943
> Radio Station KUTA, Salt
> Lake City, Utah TIME:
> 3:15 P.M. to 3:30 P.M.
>
> Script: Pvt. Virginia Brouk
>
> MUSIC (10 seconds) The Thunderer
>
> ANCC: It's STRICTLY G.I. Good afternoon ladies and gentlemen, we are about to present the second of the WAC series program, STRICTLY G.I. presented each Saturday at 3:15 P.M. over this station. SONG….
>
> BROUK: Thank you Pvt. Gellers…..that is an inspiration. Many of you women ask the question "Just what type of girls join the WAC?" Well, just take a look at your neighbors daughter ----- then add a little bit of courage, sense of responsibility, patriotism, and self-confidence to her and you will have the WAC – a member of the Women's Army Corps. By adding strength to the strength of our fighting men, we may be able to help end the war a little sooner, and help save the life of someone very dear to you.
>
> ANNC: And so we say good-bye until next time. You have been listening to STRICTLY G.I., the weekly WAC program presented each week over station KUTA at 3:15 P.M Good afternoon.

Ginny continued recruiting and was included in promotional photographs for the WAC as she showed the women of Utah who came in to enlist the equipment and gear they would be using in service.

*Ginny prepares a new WAC for duty.*

On October 2, 1943, Virginia went on air again with her radio program STRICTLY G.I. The transcript follows.[55]

> WAC Detachment
> Utah Recruiting District Headquarters
> 179 Motor Avenue, Salt Lake City, Utah
>
> RADIO BROADCAST:   Saturday, October 2, 1943
> Station KUTA
> Salt Lake City
> TIME, 15 minutes
> 3:15 P.M. to 3:30 P.M.

Music (10 seconds) fades out as announcer speaks -------
-- The Thunderer

ANNC: STRICTLY G.I. is back again for another full quarter of an hour for the purpose of informing you about the Women's Army Corps and entertaining you. During this program we hope you will relax and enjoy that much needed rest. Lt. Helen Kooles, WAC Commander of this district, has an important message for you now. Lt. Kooles, are you ready?

KOOLES: Yes I am Mr. Agee, Thank you. As you already know the ALL-STATES PLAN WAC Recruiting Program started September 7. Our offensive in this war must be sustained. To do this we must send thousands of replacements to the battlefronts and keep supply lines moving, and since women can take over many vital Army Jobs, we are calling on them to help out in an emergency. Our civilization has been built by men and women working together from the Jamestown and Plymouth colonies, through pioneer days and the era of small cities, to our modern industrial ages. Now that we are in a total war, affecting the total population, men and women must work together once more toward another Victory. The aim of this drive is to recruit women volunteers "to equal the total ballet casualties of the Army to date." We people in the state of Utah will recruit the equivalent to the number of casualties of the Army for our state alone. A special feature of this drive will be the formation of state WAC companies, so that all the girls from their own states can have their basic training together. Each state will wear a distinctive shoulder patch insignia giving the State name. We want every woman in America to feel that when the last "cease-fire" has sounded; when the Army has been mustered out; when the WACs and soldiers are free to live again in the hills plains, and cities of their native states, the women of this country again will have been true to their traditions. We have with us today, Pvt. Wally Williams, who plays the piano, and Cpl. William Fowler, who plays the guitar. Both are stationed at the Recruiting and Induction District Headquarters. Their first number will be ................. Thank you boys, that was fine.

And now Pvt. Virginia Brouk will read you a poem.

    BROUK:    (softly, with music in background)

Thank you Lt. Kooles. This poem was written by an American mother whose son is with the Armed Forces. It was written by Mona Kene West entitled "I Will Do My Part."

"Starting right now ---- I will live my life to save a man. All my waking hours I will work for the safety of this man. I need not say to anyone who the man is,
    It may be a friend or father, husband, brother or son.
    All that matters is, I shall see him before me as I work.
    I shall put forth all my effort, as if the life of this man depended on me, alone.
    As if I alone could put into his hands, the weapons to save the world.
    As if I alone made the ships, guns, tanks, and airplanes he needs.
    Before I sleep at night, I will look deep into my own conscious,
    To see if any greedy or selfish act of mine has hampered him.
    This man ---- who may be fighting in jungles or drowning in icy seas.
    To this end I will work.
    I shall not let him down."

    We will now hear .................. Played by Pvt. Williams and Cpl. Fowler. (Music.)

    Thank you again.

    BROUK:    Many of your people wonder how much a WAC really likes over-seas duty. Well, Mr. and Mrs. Bert Kinsey, of 68 Lincoln Street, Midvale, Utah, have a daughter Pvt. Elizabeth Bush in North Africa. Mrs. Kinsey has been very nice in letting us have some letters written by her daughter. And so I will read you a few paragraphs from each one. This one was written August 5, 1943 headed "Somewhere on the ocean." I quote, "Dearest Mother, dad, and Jackie, This is one of the most wonderful experiences I could ever hope to encounter. I am still pinching myself to see if I am really awake because it just does not seem possible or even real that I am where I am right now, or that I am going where I am going. The trip so far has been very pleasant, and since the food is so delicious, I would not be surprised if I had gained a few pounds already. Unquote.

The second letter is dated August 13, 1943 and it starts out with, Dearest Mother, dad, and Jackie. I quote, "We have finally arrived at the place we have been waiting to see for such a long time, and it is wonderful. We were amazed at everything we saw here in North Africa for it seems to be very different. The American soldiers we talked to said it was just like money from home to be able to see and talk to an American girl once more. We eat out of our own individual mess kits with which we wash ourselves after each meal. It certainly does cut down on K.P." [End quote.]

KOOLES: Pvt. Brouk, doesn't Elizabeth write about living in a convent?

BROUK: Yes, Mam, it says here that the convent has tile walls and floors and a veranda which overlooks the Mediterranean Sea.

KOOLES: This is cute too, Virginia. It says "we are the first WAC's that have ever been in this town, so you can imagine how much attention we are getting. We have certainly had our pictures taken so many times since we have arrived. The things we miss most are Coca-Colas and candy. But you can always get used to doing without things if you know you have to."

BROUK: Lt. Kooles, she also writes, quote, "This over-seas duty is going to be a priceless experience. If you could only see how happy and contented I am, you would have no reason in the world to worry about me. I am in no danger, whatsoever, and just think of all the things I am going to have to tell you when I get back home again." Unquote.

Shall we have some music now? Good. This time it will be ......

ANNC: You have just been listening to Lt. Helen Kooles and Private Virginia Brouk both of the Women's Army Corps and their guests Cpl. William Fowler and Private Wally Williams, at the guitar and piano, for a quarter of an hour presentation of "STRICTLY G.I." Tune in again next week at the same time, same station. Good afternoon.

On October 28, 1943, Ginny was promoted from Private to Corporal T/5 Grade.[56] By November 23, she was transferred from Salt Lake City to Provo, Utah. She spent a few weeks there doing similar jobs as she did in Salt Lake City.

What is interesting to note is that on December 19, 1943, Ginny was on the radio show Mission Tonight talking about her reasons for joining the WAC as part of the "The Air Forces Salute the WAC Day." She also discussed Robert's service, and his accident. Ginny said, "I wanted to continue the work that Bob started, and I felt that the best way to do it was to join the Women's Army Corps."[57] Lt. Langford spoke of Robert's close call with the Japanese when

*Ginny and Lt. Paul Langford On Air.*

he was strafed and injured in China in April 1942 and again elaborated on his status as a famous Flying Tiger. While emotions churned inside her chest and her heart shattered again, Ginny remained strong throughout the interview just as she had when Robert died. Photos taken of Ginny and co-host Lt. Paul Langford during the radio broadcast showed a happy Ginny.

One of the many duties Virginia had as a WAC in Utah, was writing weekly reports. Below is one example of a weekly report she wrote which detailed her duties.[58] She was required to recruit five women a week which was difficult because the Mormons did not want their women involved in the military in any capacity.

>
> ARMY SERVICE FORCES
> SCU #1965
> UTAH RECRUITING & INDUCTION DISTRICT
> Sub-station, Provo, Utah
>
> 8 January 1944
>
> SUBJECT:   Sub-station Weekly Report
>
> TO: Commanding Officer; ASF SCU #1965, Utah
>   Recruiting and Induction District Headquarters,
>   179 Motor Avenue, Salt Lake City, Utah
>
> 1.   General Recruiting Activities:

    a.    Kept in constant touch with local newspaper, Provo Herald, and transmitted all articles concerning recruiting to headquarters.

    b.    Contacted local radio station, KOVO, in reference to radio broadcast NO. 1 released from headquarters. Time was received and program was given.

    c.    Sent out letters and information to prospects:
        i.    Susie
        ii.    Esther
        iii.    Helen
        iv.    Inez

    d.    Contacted Ramola, and La Ree. Both women seem interested but want to complete this semester of school.

    e.    Contacted some women from our "dead file" of last September.

    f.    Contacted Mr. Frank Earl, from Standard Oil in regard to the 4th War Bond Drive January 18, 1944. Our services in connection with this Bond Drive were offered.

    g.    Called Mrs. H.B. Mensel, and Mrs. Hazel Clyde, both of Provo, Chairman, and assistant chairman of War bond Committee. Utmost cooperation has been promised.

    2.    Interviews:

    a.    Six prospective WACs were interviewed through this office.

    b.    Eight prospective Aviation Cade applicants were interviewed through this office.

    3.    Completed Applications:
    a.    WAC (0)
    b.    A.C. (3)

    4.    Forwarded:
    a.    WAC (0)
    b.    A.C. (3)

Since it has snowed quite heavily this past week, it was impossible to use the car in several instances. Therefore, the telephone was used. However, personal calls are always more effective.

As stated in paragraph 3, the "dead file" is being re-opened. Surprising enough prospects show a sign of interest and it is believed recruits will be obtained through this method.

For Commanding Office:
Virginia S. Brouk
Cpl. WAC. A-607863

# 8
# Going Overseas

Ginny heard a contingent of WACs was being formed to go overseas and she requested a transfer. Doing so meant she would lose her rank and have to start over at the bottom with the rank of Private. Rank and money did not matter to her. Her wish was to go overseas and be where Bob had been stationed in China or Burma. Her request was granted on February 11, 1944 for overseas duty but she was not going to the Pacific.[59] She was downgraded in rank to Private as all WACs were when they accepted overseas assignments, and returned to Fort Oglethorpe, Georgia, for six weeks of overseas training. She arrived at Fort Oglethorpe on February 22, 1944.[60]

Overseas training consisted of a refresher of what was learned in basic training and moved to additional topics such as medical care and first aid, military customs, map reading, and how to protect oneself from the enemy using slit trenches and gas masks.[61]

When training was completed, the WACs were given a short furlough to visit family before reporting to Camp Patrick Henry in Virginia. It was here on May 12, 1944, Ginny boarded the Liberty ship U.S. Army Transport (USAT) Santa Rosa, at

*Ginny ready for overseas.*

the Hampton Roads Port which was located at Camp Patrick Henry in Virginia. The ship was bound for a destination unknown to the troops, but ultimately it was supposed to be Suez, Africa.[62]

The USAT Santa Rosa was built in 1932 by Federal Shipbuilding & Dry Dock in Kearny, New Jersey. She was a luxury ship with outside first class cabins with private baths; a gym and swimming pool, and something unusual for a ship in her day, a dining room with a ceiling that could be opened.[63] She was called to serve her country in 1941 and operated by the Grace Line, Inc. and War Shipping Administration.

Ginny wrote, "We were a group of 361 WACs, and 4,000 paratroopers were on the boat with us."[64] The ship was destined for Africa but due to reversals suffered by General Stillwell, the ship stopped first in Bagnoli, Italy. Ginny recalled her time on the ship in her memoir, stating,

"Our trip across the Atlantic was very smooth. I ate hardboiled eggs morning, noon, and night so as not to get seasick, and it worked. I was fine and up and about during the whole voyage. My five roommates on the other hand spent most of their time in their bunks. All five took turns being sick. I said it was a smooth trip, and it really was, but we did have days of rather constant high rolling waves and that constant roll set some people off – to misery and bed. You see, we ate our meals standing up alongside of counters. One day it was very stormy and the waves were so high the boat rolled and rolled from side to side. Trying to eat and hold onto rolling trays without losing your footing took quite a bit of skill. I remember eating the hardboiled egg of one of the G.I.'s after he had suddenly left the counter. I collected several more eggs from empty trays before I left the cleared out mess hall. They saved my tummy.

We had two sets of three tiered hammocks in our small room in the hull of the boat. I slept on the lowest bunk. Had a torpedo hit us, we would never have suffered. We would have been dead before the next wave would have come along. Only once did I wonder why

I volunteered for this experience. It did scare me when we were ordered to sit side by side in a narrow hallway and were told not to move a muscle, be quiet, no whispering, no coughing, and no cigarette lite. We were informed our arrival into the Mediterranean Sea had just been announced by the Germans, and that their sub was somewhere beneath us. All our engines suddenly stopped and everything was silent. We just floated. All I could hear was the thumping of my heart. I have no idea how long we were in this mode, but to all of us aboard, it seemed forever. The rest of our convoy – our protectors, were far ahead of us and reached the final destination safely. How did we get so far behind? Engine trouble. So we were now alone and had to defend ourselves. It was not supposed to be that way, but it was. Nevertheless we were stunned. We knew what was going on."[65]

*At times the ships in the convoy did get hit, as photographed by a G.I. on board the USAT Santa Rosa.*

The cruise overseas was not completely terrible for all involved. Some did get sick and there was the sub scare, but good times were had along the way. Ginny recalled,

"On the lighter side, we did have some good times on board. The paratroopers had their own band, and so we attended several dances. With 4,000 young men around 361 women, we had nothing to worry about. We could not find time to be lonely. The conversation was usually, 'Hi – I'm so and so, where are you from?'

We had fashion shows and I modeled my own two-piece bathing suit. The soldiers were told they could take pictures of the models. Some did pretty good. Now I know why the military always gave the G.I.'s salt peter!

*WACs in Naples. Ginny is on the truck.*

Our contingent was scheduled for a Mideast docking but at the last moment General Stillwell suffered reverses in Northern Africa. Therefore, we were temporarily assigned to duty in Bagnoli, Italy, a suburb of Naples. We entered the center of town in trucks, 361 women. What a sight it must have been! We were housed in a building where Mussolini often spoke and our three daily meals were eaten on steps along the laundry lines. There was no mess hall around."[66]

*GIs eating on the setps in Naples.*

"We arrived just as Rome fell and everything was in shambles. Refugees were all over the place. Most homes were not fit to live in. Everything was make-shift. We all pitched in and did our best.

*Building where Mussolini often spoke where the WACs were housed.*

Our building did not have any glass in the window panes so the nights were really cold. No heat, no sheets, no pillows; just a cot and one brown woolen blanket. The Germans had camouflaged our building to look like a forest from an American fighter plane. We were the first WACs to go straight from the states to a combat zone. The day we arrived we were 45 minutes from the front lines."[67]

> Virginia wrote many letters home after she went overseas. The original letters are gone, but Virginia has a file of military papers and included in them was a set of typed letters. Her mother typed many of the letters she sent home which begin in June of 1944 and end in January 1945. The letters that still exist are scattered throughout this story with the story of her life she wrote in her memoir. GIs were not usually allowed to say where they were so the letters start "Somewhere in ...." with a date.

*"Somewhere in Italy"*
*June 1944*

After a most pleasant trip, we have arrived somewhere in Italy. The voyage across was really wonderful. At times one could not realize a war was on, for one had male companionship and entertainment galore; such as dances, movies and romance.

Oh no, I never got seasick. In fact, I never felt better in my life. I can't kick about the food as yet. Of course, milk is a drink of the past. Therefore, I have to try to settle for wine. The water is so heavily chlorinated that it doesn't make drinking a pleasure.

Yes, I am able to tell you, that it's perfectly beautiful here. That's about all. The views around here even surpass the beauty of Utah; and I thought that was impossible. I am speaking of course about the terrain. This place has been heavily bombed and there are signs of war everywhere. Beautiful homes, cathedrals, etc. are in a mass of destruction. The people are clothed very poorly, and I am certain they haven't seen a shower for ages. One can see young boys and girls, as well as adults, stand around and beg for food and cigarettes. In fact you can almost buy anything you want with a package of cigarettes.

Their language is positively a nightmare to me. My Swiss isn't getting me anywhere. You know, how capable I am of handling American money, so you can readily imagine what a mess I can get into here. I try to use the good old sign language but at times I only get a blank stare in return.

We girls have a lovely place to stay at now. We sleep on cots and roll ourselves in blankets. What are those things called sheets? By the way, I must tell you, we have servants to scrub our floors, shoes, latrines, and clean up. Not bad, eh? We don't have any hot water, but are very thankful to have it cold. Days have elapsed when we have not seen a drop, and anything is welcome now.

We discovered a new easy method in which to iron shirts and skirts without our iron or electricity. Just wash clothes and then press them dry with the palms of the hand in the sun. It only takes hours, but then one looks quite stunning.

Quaint people, quaint customs, destruction and suffering sum up my experiences and eye-witness scenes thus far. Truly a novel in itself already.

Since we haven't any electricity, we live like little chicks. "early to bed, early to rise."

P.S. I saw the Rock of Gibraltar, but by jinks, there was no Prudential Life Insurance sign on it. "Ain't that something!"[68]

\*\*\*\*\*

*Ginny in the Naples aera with GIs.*

"To get away from the war torn areas after work, we usually got a group together, hopped on a military truck and went up the mountainside to a lovely retreat. There we relaxed, had some drinks and danced. My escort in Italy was a Lieutenant. I met him on the boat. In the states, non-coms [non-commissioned personnel] could not date officers, but overseas there were no rules. Bob and I were in Naples. When I went to Cairo, he went to France and I never heard from him again. He was a paratrooper.[69]

While in Naples we drove to Pompeii and saw Mt. Vesuvius which had erupted just a few months before, and was still emitting smoke and tossing large clumps of lava in every direction. What a breathtaking sight. Lethal yes, but beautiful.[70]

*Mount Vesuvius.*

*Going Overseas* 79

By now Rome was completely taken over by the Americans. Thus began the second invasion. We WACs were sent to Taranto via Salerno. We arrived in Taranto and Boarded the Polish ship, Batory which was manned by the British. The ship also carried Indian troops heading back to India. We left port and traveled to Alexandria, Egypt."[71]

*Alexandria, Egypt's shoreline.*

### *"Somewhere in Egypt"*
### *June 1944*

I am now thoroughly convinced that I am enjoying a world observation tour sponsored by the Women's Army Corps.

Whatever comes my way you can be assured will be well taken in and remembered for future use. We were only a 45 minute ride from the front lines. That in itself should explain quite a bit. Upon our arrival we were informed, that Germany announced our safe arrival and also the correct number in our unit over their radio.

I must admit that we were not wholly responsible for the Invasion, nor the falling of Rome. However, being so close to it and having arrived shortly before it began, one could accidentally give us some credit. We saw the Italian evacuees from Rome pass through Naples. It was truly a sad sight.

It is unbelievable how the poorer class of people live. The word "exist" would more accurately describe the situation. They do not wear shoes and their clothing is just a combination of material tied together in order to cover parts of the body. Apparently they have never been taught the uses of water for they certainly make no attempt to use it.

Most of the homes must have been lovely 'villas' at one time. However, a great percentage can no longer be placed in that category. Walls of the homes have been bombed out and much of the interior destroyed. No doubt, in time, the ruins will be removed. It's been too early thus far.

I visited Naples quite frequently. A friend and myself attended the San Carlo Opera and saw the performance of 'La Traviata.' What thrilled me the most was that we sat in the King's box. We felt rather important beneath the clusters of gold leaves and velvet-red drapery. Gold walls, mirrors, and velvet drapery with oil painted murals make up the interior of the Opera house. The auditorium has one main floor and the box seats set vertically along the sides and back wall; very strange, yet very comfortable and beautiful.

On several occasions we had dinner at a place called El Rotando. It was similar to our Olson's and situated on a mountain top. The views from there were gorgeous. Along with the beautiful sunsets we could view lovely scenery of hills, mountains, lowlands and bodies of water. A few areas of destruction within range of our vision reminded us of our mission from time to time. At this place we had a steak dinner with potatoes, salad, champagne and vini. In the background a three piece orchestra played waltzes. Mix champagne and Vermouth for a delicious drink.

We also had the opportunity to visit Pompeii. We saw parts of the city that had been excavated. The layout of their streets and their construction of homes was quite amazing. Mt. Vesuvius erupted several months ago and streams of lava 35 to 60 feet deep covered the remains of Pompeii. To date some of the city ruins are still covered.

One Sunday I went sailing and saw the Isle of Capri. I couldn't possibly find enough descriptive words to describe the scenery. I just sat and stared in amazement. It is truly unbelievable how much beauty there is in this world, and how little we appreciate it.

We watched the fisherman dry and fix their nets. We saw the street markets that resemble our Maxwell street. We saw American, English, Russian, Polish, and Indian troops. We also went for horse and buggy rides in town.

The people beg, beg, beg. Diseases are prevalent, but no one seems to know what to do about them. So they are just taken for granted. One wonders, at times, whether it is being Christian to give an infant a start in such a life.

I also got a glimpse of Salerno, Casino, and nearby neighboring towns. Some towns had been flattened down to street level and not even an ant can be seen around the place.

At times, I felt like a debutante. We girls received invitations after invitation to dances and parties. Refreshments were always served and good times were had by all.

Turning to the more serious aspect, we visited the base hospital where we met boys returning directly from the battlefront. In fact, some had not received medical attention before we fed them. Conversation always began with 'where are you from?' and I heard varied remarks. However, at this writing I cannot voice my opinion on the reaction of war on these wounded soldiers.

Our voyage from Italy to our present home was quite novel. We had four full-sized meals daily with tablecloths, silverware, and plates. We had four girls to a room with hot running water, white sheets, full length mirrors and writing facilities. The trip was very enjoyable.

Cloud formations and crimson-red sunsets with beautiful white-capped waves filled my heart with contentment. Many hours were spent reminiscing and my mind always came to dwell finally upon the thought that thus far I've had quite a full, thrilling life and hope that this present cycle of my life will add to my previous adventures.

"After a long, hot, miserable ride from Alexandria, we arrived in Cairo. The coal driven old train blew all the black soot into our faces because there was no glass to cover the window frames. All 361 girls had sore throats and dirty nostrils.[72]

*Ginny traveled by train from Alexandria to Cairo.*

Our contingent under the command of Major Josephine Dyer, arrived at Camp Huckstep, a desert base located 10 miles from Cairo proper. Our unit was divided into two groups. Group I – USAFIME known as WAC Detachment Headquarters, Cairo Military District. Group II – MESCA known as WAC Detachment Headquarters Mesca-Huckstep. I was assigned to Group I.

Our 99 WACs plus myself arrived at the "New Hotel" located in the center of Cairo. My roommates were: Leora (Fergie) Ferguson – IL; Evelyn Seims – NY; Julia Hogan – CT; Anna Honas – PA; Magdalene Perrou – CA. Magdalene and I became best friends and have remained so to this writing [2010.]"[73]

*Our contingent under the command of Major Josephine Dyer, arrived at Camp Huckstep, a desert base located 10 miles from Cairo proper.*

*The WACs of Camp Huckstep.*

### "Somewhere in Egypt"
### June 1944

While sitting in a desert heat of 125° one afternoon, I was pleasantly surprised with 33 letters from the States. You can't imagine how happy I was. I have them before me and my bed looks like a cyclone struck this place.

Roselyn and Rose are my next door bunk mates and we get along famously. It may be because the heat makes one feel far from energetic. The afternoons are almost unbearable, but then we were informed that it reaches 167 in the fall. By that time, we'll either be acclimated or else will be another added attraction in the land of Cleopatra – mummies (American style.)

Our camp is rather nice, strictly G.I. We have brick barracks with modern conveniences including two washing machines. I am also able to use my iron.

This country is unique – unique in many respects – climate, terrain, population, and architecture. I'll describe each separately so that you'll understand what I mean by my statement. The climate appears to be very dry, the weather as I stated before, extremely hot. Our hair has a tendency to get brittle from the heat and sun.

Sand and more sand is quite noticeable. Few hills of sand, lowlands of sand, paths with sand, food with sand, clothes with sand and beds of sand constitutes the beauty of nature here. (Ain't that something?) I can't say much about the green trees, flowers or shrubbery for I haven't seen any. Just sand. Remember.

I had the opportunity to visit Cairo some time ago. That trip opened my eyes to many, many things. The architecture of the buildings is definitely like our modern homes. Now, I can't seem to discover whether we copied the mode from the Egyptians or whether they took it from us. The city is very clean and beautiful (that is, the richer side of town.) The streets are full with flowers, trees and benches in the center of the roads. Street-cars run quite frequently, but no one would want to enter them. I'll explain why later. Each home is colored beautifully. Light blue, pink or cream are the prominent shades. Each home has a terrace with lovely flowers and vines growing along the side walls.

*Ginny on a camel.*

*Going Overseas* 85

Their backyards would be our Columbus Park setup.

Vegetation and irrigation is good however primitive. Camels come into the picture here. I had the opportunity to visit the pyramids which I thoroughly enjoyed. We took a camel ride through the citadels, the Mamelouks Tomb, the Pyramid of Quizeh and the Sphinx. I have many pictures of all the places I have been to and I'll send them to you as soon as I've permission to do so.

Now, I would like to bring up the subject of population. Please bear in mind that I am not exaggerating in the least bit. I can hardly believe what I have to write myself. The people are divided into four classes:

1. Professional class: these people have some money, live in the sections I have described in the second paragraph, page 2. These people are cultured and dress modernly. However they are more European than American. Many have traveled and speak several languages.

2. The artisan class of people are located in the cities – such as shopkeepers, craftsmen, and skilled workers. They are very patient individuals and are used to soldiers.

3. This type consists of the peasant-farmers and are called the "Fellaheen." These people are poor, very poor. He eats little beyond bread, beans, onions and very occasional mutton at feasts. I can't understand

*Ginny on left in Cairo, Egypt.*

it, but they do seem to be contented. I'd put them in our low class of people at home.

4. Last we have the semi-nomadic tribesmen of the desert, known as a WOG. At first I had to laugh at these people's costumes, then I felt itchy and dirty and finally I felt sorry for them. However, I still have to stare. Imagine an oddly shaped creature walk the streets with trays of pies or orange crates on his head. Add to this scene thousands of flies over this figure plus unbelievable odors. Along with this odor are spots from food and grease and spots from lack of education in personal hygiene. The human form is draped with rags from head to foot. The women dress in black veils covering their heads, face and body. On a few only the eyes show. A black veil designates a woman is married.

Within a short time I learned the WOGS dress the way they do because of the "hot sun and heat." The long white sleeved nightgowns are called Galabias and keep the WOGS cool and safe from sunburn. (Not such a dumb idea afterall.)

The poorer sections of the town are indescribable. The width of the streets are no wider than 12 feet. On either side, there are large stone buildings, cluttered up with old rags and canvass covering. On the streets can be seen (countless) counters where merchandise is sold. One street consists of meat, while another specializes in pastries, etc. It is not unusual to see half a cow hanging in the center of the road and have the people walk around or under it. Nine out of ten bump against it and, of course, the meat is not covered.

*Cairo farmers market.*

Then too, I saw a woman nurse a child on the sidewalk and sell watermelons to a customer at the same time. Across from her, not more than 12 feet away, a young boy about 10 years of age, decided to go to the bathroom by the curb.

One cannot quite realize that in this day and age it is possible for human beings to live so primitively and filthy. Words in history and geography books never made too much of an impression on me, but now that I am actually seeing these things, I'm wide eyed and spellbound!

The Prince and Princess of Egypt came to visit Camp Huckstep. She [the Princess] was exceptionally pleasant and looked like any American. If I'm not mistaken I believe she was educated in England.

100 of us were transferred from Camp Huckstep and assigned to duty in Cairo proper. We were assigned to quarters at the New Hotel, 10 blocks away from the Military Dispensary, our work place. 261 women stayed at Camp Huckstep.

"I worked for Major Alder, an Army Nurse in the Medical Dispensary. WAC Lillian St. Martin was in the same office as were G.I.'s Luster, Revise, and Jimmy. Magdalene was a dental assistant a few doors from my medical records office. Our area was the 38th General Hospital – USAFIME – Dispensary.

My job was to deliver the patients records to the correct location after having recorded the information for the doctors. I, also, had to notify the next of kin in the event of a soldier's death or missing in action. That obviously bothered me.

Our billet was 10 blocks away from the dispensary so we had good walks back and forth."[74]

"One day I forgot to remove my pen from my shirt pocket as I was getting ready to go back to the hotel. The work day was over and

I was to meet Magdalene and discuss some G.I.'s medical recording problem with her. I was busy gathering papers and never thought about my fountain pen. Normally, I knew better.

As we were walking and talking, a WOG passed by us, and then suddenly turned around, knocked me down onto the sidewalk, and just as suddenly disappeared. With the help of many chattering Arabs, I was again on my feet still trying to figure out what happened. You guessed it. That native stole my pen, and ripped my shirt pocket "to boot.""[75]

"Another day which happened to be a Sunday afternoon, I took a sightseeing tour with six other WACs. We went to see "old-city-Cairo" – not the best part of town. We did have a guide and were told to stay close together and so we felt considerably safe. All went well for hours as we walked up and down the narrow streets, in and out of the tiny shops and tried to make eye contact and communicate with the natives.

Suddenly a woman screamed. I turned around to see what was happening when someone grabbed my left wrist and tried to bend my arm behind my back. I saw a man with a machete in his hand. Apparently, he was going to cut off my wrist or fingers to get at my engagement and wedding rings. I did not wait to find out. I just began to scream louder and louder over and over again. He vanished in the crowd. The five girls and I were a wreck for a few days, and everyone at our dispensary was made aware of it. I was by far not the only WAC who wore wedding/engagement rings. Why me?"[76]

"It was so hot (125°-130°) during the summer that we washed our uniforms by hand, and then went up on the roof of the hotel, laid them on the roof to damp dry. We then kept pressing our uniforms with hot bricks since we did not have access to an iron. The end result was fine. The process was just awkward.."[77]

### *"Somewhere in Palestine"*
### *30 June 1944*

A most unusual and exciting incident came my way a few days ago. I had the opportunity to fly with six other girls and a publicity staff from my home base to Palestine. We had a marvelous time sightseeing and had our pictures taken at various places. These photographers took movies of our contingent when we landed in Italy and carried the story of our daily adventures thru to our present destination. Within two or three months, the public in the States should be able to view them as "news shorts" in theaters or "half hour added attraction runs". Keep your eyes and ears open, you might be able to find one-fourth of the family smiling at you.

*On the plane to Palestine.*

Now about my trip. Truly another adventure. We flew in a D.C. 3 bomber over the desert and the Suez Canal. You know, it really was a strange feeling. There I was sitting on a metal seat, strapped in with a parachute at my feet. Before me I could see the radio man, alongside his instruments, which seemed to me a mightily complicated affair. At my side were the pilots – 1st and Co. I spoke to them frequently and thus obtained enough information to make the trip more worthwhile.

They even let me listen in the earphones when we landed. Because the trip was not of a military nature ( a mission) nor a direct and regular route, I'm quite certain it would not be harmful to tell you we flew 138 miles an hour at 5000 ft. altitude. It was a beautiful sunny day from the cockpit and I could see clouds; white, fluffy, soft looking clouds which took different shapes and forms as we flew through, over and under them. While flying under them I could see the desert. Never could I explain to you the queer sensation that came over me when I beheld that sight. There, beneath me, thousands of feet away, was the desert I read so much about. The desert, I thought, would be deadly and hot looking. Instead, it looked exceptionally beautiful, colorful and cool. That, believe me, can only be from a distance. The sand had ripples from the wind and formed various figures. The sun shining through the soft clouds added the light and shade and as the rays hit the sand it glittered in several shades, ranging from a soft yellow, orange, yellow to a dark red and maroon.

Suddenly, a long snakey dark blue affair could be seen winding its way along the desert. As we approached the mirage, it took form of the Suez Canal. The contrast in colors would make a gorgeous slide. The canal seemed rather narrow, but then I imagine the altitude had something to do with it.

As we neared the end of our pleasant journey, my ears began to hum and the ship began to dance amidst the clouds. By the time the bomber decided to try a jive number my tummy decided to rebel. After disembarking, I found it rather difficult to manipulate, however, only for a few moments.

We stayed at the Y.M.C.A. Strange, isn't it? It's a beautifully modern building with very well kept

*YMCA in Palestine.*

flowered park opening grounds before it. Eliminating the heat and inhabitants, plus the odor, one could almost believe, they were somewhere in the states. Remember, I said almost. Our rooms were lovely, kept clean and neat. We had room service, hot water, and laundry accommodations. Meals weren't American but I managed to keep that empty feeling from sneaking up on me.

During the day we went sightseeing and had our pictures taken. As I mentioned before, that was the reason for this trip.

Among the most impressive sights during these days was our visit to Bethlehem and Jerusalem. Here one could realize easily that worldly advancement is unheard of and that religion not only plays an important part in the people's life, but the one and only part. They live the Bible. Men, women, and children enter the Temple and pray, enter the stores, pray, the streets, pray. They are all barefooted and wear long white gowns. Many men have long hair and beards.

*Ginny on the right kneeling in the Church of the Nativity*

While visiting Bethlehem, I saw the "Manger" in which Christ was laid and which has been rebuilt of marble by the crusaders. It is located in a beautiful temple. I also saw the cave of Christ's Nativity. A silver star marks the actual spot of His birth. Surrounding the place are candles by the hundreds beautifully lit with marble columns in the background. We also saw the birthplace of David, Tomb of Rachel, The Church of St. Catherine, and the Grotto of St. Jerome, where he lived and translated the Bible from Hebrew to Latin.

In Jerusalem, I went to the Wailing Wall. It is a remainder of the Wall that surrounded the Temple area built by Herod I. It is looked upon as the most sacred place to the Jewish people. This wall is located in the poorest section of Jerusalem. One begins at the top of some stairs and it is almost a nightmare to reach it. Along this wall are blocks indented about one foot, on which the people or worshippers lay their Bible.

*The Wailing Wall*

They then throw a long white robe over their heads and bodies and tie a black cord around their neck and over their left shoulder and waist. After this preparation they stoop over slightly and begin to pray. With a bible written in Hebrew language held about two inches from their faces (the people's eyes are terribly impaired due to diseases both from filth and venereal diseases.) They begin to shout and yell to the top of their lungs. In between breaths, they hum and sing and then they go into tantrums again. Picture taking is against their religion and since I really appreciate their feelings toward that subject I didn't have the heart. So I didn't snap a picture, however I did pick a few photos up in town for a few Piastres.

The Via Doloroza (Way of suffering) road through which Jesus Christ carried the Cross to Calvary was an impressive sight. The road has 14 stations of the Cross; 9 on the way up and 4 on Calvary. The 15th is the Holy Sepulcher. Every Friday afternoon, a procession takes place by the Catholics. The street is very, very narrow with bridges overhead from one house

*The Via Doloroza*

to another. Little sun reaches this area, so it is rather damp and musty looking.

The Church of All Nations impressed me the most. It's absolutely gorgeous and beautiful, a hundred times over. The twelve interior domes as well as the floor are constructed of mosaic stone. The windows are of alabaster. It stands next to the Garden of Gethsemane, where I picked the passion flower. If you recall that flower only blooms in the Garden of Gethsemane during certain months of the year. It's a beautifully purpose based flower and resembles our aster. On top of the base, which represents the holy wreath, are five yellow leaves or petals in a star-like form emerging from the center. These petals indicate the five nails with which Christ was nailed to the Cross. Directly above the petals are three black round-like fuzzy petals which represent the Cross. Christ prayed daily in this Garden.

*The Church of All Nations*

The Citadel was quite an interesting place to see. If I remember correctly, that was where General Allenby (On Dec 1717) Declared the deliverance of the city of Jerusalem by the British Troops.

As we moved on to Mount Olive, we could see the panorama of Jerusalem. It was an impressive sight, I must admit a strange sensation went through me as I stood in these Temples. A feeling of guilt entered my mind as I stood in these sacred places and I vowed over and over again to myself that I'd try to live what these people really stand for. Living a life so full, worldly and modern, as we have, it doesn't take much to make one forget the basis of complete happiness. However, it hits you so horribly fast and hard when you see these people and their sincere belief in Christ.

The terrain of Palestine is unusually lovely. It's hilly and quite good for vegetation. However not much is done beside praying and sheepherding.

In the evening, we went nightclubbing in town. We discovered a cute little place which was in bounds to Allied Troops. There we danced with British troops, drank Hungarian liquor (please do not inquire where the latter came from) and discussed war and politics. I'll still take our own G.I.'s any day.

We flew home in the Colonel's private plane, a Lockheed 61, and had a grand smooth trip. The adventure was all too short since there were so many more interesting places to visit. We had a good time and found a lot of things back at camp, which I write about in my next letter.

*"Somewhere in Egypt"*
*7 July 1944*

I imagine by this time you are rather curious as to what I am doing; that is in the line of work. I'll try to enlighten you on that subject now.

I am working in the Medical Section, Personnel Department, and doing something, I feel, is really worthwhile. It is a much bigger task than I thought it would be. However, at times I get slightly depressed. You see, I handle the sick, wounded, and death reports for the entire Middle East sections including battle casualties. By the time you complete a case, you know the patient quite well, and if things don't turn out well you can't help but think of his nearest kin. It hits home often. I'll just have to try and look at it as a job and only as such I guess.

A few days ago, some of our girls and me left the camp where we were stationed, and were transferred into town. At the present writing, we are living in a hotel with three or four girls to a room. As yet, I can't decide whether the move was to our advantage or not. The desert was not too appealing at times, but then this awfully smelly, filthy town isn't much better. The heat penetrates in both places, so one just can't win. At any rate, I am a city girl again enjoying Egypt's insect and flea bites seeing more filth and dirt and learning rapidly about the customs of other people; and above all being oh so happy to be an American.

Getting back to my living quarters.

We do have an elevator in the hallway and since we live on the third floor it comes in handy at times. I say at times, because it usually doesn't work and decides to stop somewhere between floors. We have a large room with two windows covered with nettings, four beds and two dressers. Oh yes, I must not forget to tell you that we have a spittoon too. (No comments, please.)

Our daily walk of 10 blocks to and from work brings forth many a laugh at the natives, a frown of disgust, and a sigh of relief that we have a home to go back to someday.

For instance:

Yesterday a "Wog" [In the 1940s, anyone in the Middle East, Africa, and those areas with darker skin was referred to as a Wog.] was walking down the street carrying her baby boy. (They carry their babies on their shoulder, one leg in front and the other in back, and the baby hangs on to the mother's head.) Anyway, the child apparently had a sore eye and honestly, I'm not exaggerating in the least when I say there were 15 to 20 big dirty, filthy flies on this boy's eye. In fact, we couldn't see the eye itself. Neither the child nor the mother made any attempt to remove them. My breakfast didn't settle too well after that.

A few blocks further, my little eyes almost popped out again. This time it was a 'WOG ' walking down the street in his usual attire (a filthy night gown) pulling a cow behind him. Suddenly, he stopped and decided to milk this cow (mind you, in the middle of main street.) After doing so, he began to yell in Arabic. Few Wogs came to buy the milk and then he went on his way.

These Egyptians catch on quickly. The other day while walking home two Wogs dressed in purple satin gowns and white dinner jackets winked at me and gave me that look. It was all I could do not to laugh at these men. Honestly, they are strange.

Oh yes, while passing a home I saw a boy take his horse out of the front door, I stood there and waited for a camel but apparently the place wasn't large enough. The Wogs walk in the streets and let the cows and camels walk on the sidewalks. Me? I run in between the whole works.

While waiting for a Gheri one evening, a woman came up to me, lifted her black veil and began to speak. I watched her closely and noticed that she was tattooed below the nose and her chin. Since I couldn't understand her and realized she was serious, I tried my level best to make out what she was trying to tell me. Lo and behold to make a long story short, she tried to sell me her baby for a few Piastres. I had the darndest time trying to make her realize I didn't want her child. It was cute, but then there is a limit to things you know.

My, my what adventures! Please remember all this is accompanied by such pleasant odors as dried horse manure, dead animals, spoiled food and open latrines. Ah me, for a bottle of perfume.

After seeing these people wash their feet in buckets of water daily, I became rather inquisitive. No it couldn't be cleanliness, I said to myself and to be sure it wasn't. Each time before the WOGs pray they have to dip their feet in water. (They pray five times a day.)

It's so funny to watch the men work. They have to pin up their gowns in order to be able to move around. They take the back of this gown and pin it up in front between their legs. Needless to say what they look like.

Another thing, you haven't any idea how difficult it is to pass a fruit store or a pastry shop without buying a single thing. The oranges, peaches, pies, cookies, soft drink and ice cream look so inviting, but are so contaminated with germs that we are absolutely forbidden to purchase food. We do have our G.I meals, but then one does like in between snacks you know.

*Coffee salesman*

Speaking of contamination. Did you know that if a person falls into the Nile River he or she has to have eleven types of inoculations? It's an insect's paradise.

I must tell you all about the weddings and funerals here. When a young couple decides to marry, they are separated for 90 days from the date of their wedding to the 91st day. After the 91st day, there is a large reunion party at which time only the bride, bridegroom and MEN in town may attend. From that time on, the wife wears a black veil. Before that time she wears a white veil if she's under 25 years of age.

Their funerals are stranger yet. In the first place, they hire professional wailers or moaners. At a rich funeral, the body is placed in a beautifully gold covered carriage with a glass body. Flowers draped along the wheels and top of the carriage add to it. From ten to twelve horses draped in white pull this carriage. However, at a poor funeral people walk. The casket is mummy shaped and placed on the Wogs head and carried to the burial place. Hired moaners walk directly behind the body. I have never seen a woman attend a funeral yet, but I can't say they aren't permitted to do so. I don't know.

At the cemetery, they unload the body. You see, the coffin is a family possession and they carry it back home again. If the body falls "head up" the person goes to heaven. If, however, the person falls "feet up" and "head down" he or she goes to hell. [The bodies were carried in the coffin to a large grave where the coffin was turned on its side to allow the body to roll out. This allowed for the determination of heaven or hell after it fell.]

In some sections of this place, the burial place is right in their own home. Once a month they visit the dead and take all the food they possibly can with them. They sit down alongside the grave and eat the food and tell the dead everything that happened to them during the past month. This goes on for two or three days and then they return to their homes. Friday is their Sabbath day.

Prices are atrocious and inflation is present to the n'th degree. It's about 4-1.

A 'Lerner' $7.99 dress sells for $74 or 18 lbs.
A slip is $17.00
A De Soto Automobile costs $3,000.00 while a car license is $400. Tires are plentiful and there is no gas rationing at all.
One bar of Lux soap costs .60 cents. One dime store lipstick $1.00. Coty's powder $3.60 and $1.20 a roll of film. I have a cute story to tell you about this film situation. I brought two rolls in to be developed at 'Kodak' and spoke with the salesman for a few moments. He's Egyptian but spoke English rather well. I finally inquired about film. They are permitted to sell two rolls to a customer only at 14 Piastres a piece or .56 cents a roll. He gave me four rolls for .56 cents (altogether.) Imagine.

The cheapest permanent is $25.00.

I haven't learned much in the way of speaking but I can write "I love you." Read it backwards.

I am doing well as far as my weight is concerned. Haven't gained a pound though. Most of us have diarrhea. It's quite prevalent in tropical climates. A tummy ache doesn't faze us anymore. Nor do bites of any kind. If we pampered ourselves every time we find a different kind of bite, we'd be crying morning, noon, and night.

I haven't heard from anyone at all since the 13th of last month. Since no one else heard I won't worry too much, but I hope everything is fine at home. Does my mail come through? I have been writing long letters frequently. We'll use them as a diary someday. Glad to have such a grand family to come home to. Lucky me.

***"Somewhere in Egypt"***
***21 July 1944***

While lying on my bed resting this afternoon I heard a beautiful concert. It reminded me so much of our Sunday afternoons and the Philharmonic. I thought of Ruthie and how beautifully she plays and hope that she is going on with her music and does not give it up now.

When I spoke to Mr. Sandusky last May, if you remember, he told me to look up his son if I'd ever land in Egypt. Well, to make a long story short, I met him quite by accident at the dispensary while he was bathing a sore finger. A few evenings later my girlfriends and I went to a party at his home. He really has a set up. But then he is two ranks higher than Bob was. We had a lovely time talking about Chicago, Western and Cicero. He's married and has a little boy.

I spent one afternoon bicycle riding and as a result have a beautiful tan. This Egyptian sun penetrates rapidly. I rode an English bike with the brakes at the handle bar and had to ride through heavy traffic before I reached the part of town I wanted to photograph. I could just picture me in a situation similar to the one daddy had in Switzerland. However, fate was with me and all ended up well, though I am certain I aged years.

Speaking of Switzerland. I met a young Swiss woman who is a Governess for an Egyptian family. She came here nine years ago and because of the war has been unable to return home. We spoke Swiss together for quite some time and since she hails from Bern. I had no difficulty in understanding her. She claims I speak well but with an American accent. She invited me to a Swiss meeting, banquet and dance. I can hardly wait.

The other evening we were privileged to hear Lily Pons. She sang beautifully and I most certainly enjoyed her concert under the stars and moon. I must add that the nights are perfect here, in fact I must have acclimated myself already, because I am feeling fine and enjoying it all immensely.

I was very happy to have received your letter today dated 10 July 1944. I'll answer your questions best I can.

In the first place, we all left Italy and are all in Egypt. Since then we have divided – some are in town and others in camps. You know where I am. In my previous letter, I wrote you about my work. I like it more and more each day.

I have a grand collection of pictures now. I'll put them in a book and send them home someday.

By the way, has anything been cut out of my letters? Just curious.

Oh, I must tell you about the lovely boat ride I took the other evening. Six of us got a phonograph with records, a sailboat and took a moonlight cruise down the Nile. It was simply lovely.

We are still experiencing blackouts and with the Balkan affair at stake one never knows. This is our destination until......

I received your other letters last week. All are so very much appreciated; believe me.

Well, my darlings, it's 10 P.M. now and time to get ready for bed. 5:30 comes around rather quickly. It's 1 P.M. in Chicago now. Daddy and Ruthie are both working, while Granny and Mommy are talking it over, over a cup of coffee. Strange world isn't it? Good nite and all my love to you.

***"Somewhere in Egypt"***
***27 July 1944***

A few little tears, a heavily filled heart, and a wandering mind were the effects of receiving the two most beautifully written letters from my loved ones.

At this present writing, I have a somewhat strange feeling; a feeling I am quite certain you will be able to share with me. Danger amidst the deep dark sea still prevails, while worldwide attention is focused on war torn, bloody continents. Less than a month after we enjoyed a most restful, uneventful trip aboard a beautiful ship, fate struck and as a result that ship no longer sails the high seas. Since this fact is well known and has been announced publically, I wouldn't be surprised if you already know. Most of us became so well acquainted with the Polish crew members that we feel the loss of their lives greatly.

Since it is quite impossible for me to write in detail about my work, the setup in general, the war and its affects politically and economically in this Theater, I find very little, if anything to discuss outside my daily social activities. Therefore, I do hope you will not maintain the thought that yours truly just plays for a living here. There is work, and plenty of it, but a discussion on its contents will just have to wait. The political angle is more interesting than one could imagine; however that too will have to be placed in the future fire-side-chat category. Too bad.

I must inform you of my latest pastime. It is a hobby I hope to develop on Lake Michigan with the rest of my family. At the present time, I am enjoying it along the Nile – yes somewhere along the Nile; though its beauty is far surpassed by our own lake, I have become greatly interested in sailing. Seeing the little boat tilt from one side to another, sitting at an angle not too comfortable and watching the white sail away in the breeze against the blue, blue background of the lovely sky, is so picturesque; and the fact that you are guiding it single handed makes it doubly fascinating and thrilling.

During our spare evenings we often attend an outside cinema. They are quite novel. The audience sits under the stars and the moon among some beautiful trees. The talkies are in English, while directly beneath the screen can be seen the Arabic print. Below that is the French language. They have two intermissions and sell cold drinks and ice cream, which of course we G.I.'s dare not buy and eat.

The other evening a friend and myself were sitting in a little garden listening to some soft sweet music. Suddenly, we were interrupted by some Wog who wanted to sell us a pair of socks. We told him to go away and then continued our conversation. Within a short period of time we were interrupted again and again. Each time a Wog had something to sell but when one tried to sell me a watch that looked like Big Gen and sounded like a steam engine, well that was the payoff!

Ann Sheridan made a personal appearance tour through the C.B.I. and M.E.S.C. theaters of war and so we were fortunate in seeing her. I wasn't too elated after seeing her. I still maintain a photograph can make a person.

If you remember in my last letter I mentioned that I met a Swiss lady. She introduced me to a Mrs. Gausser and the three of us had dinner one evening. This Mrs. Gausser comes from Bern and Biel and speaks just like Granny. We got along famously. Tuesday, the 1st of August, I am attending their doings and will write about them in my next letter. We had "Merengue" for dessert. They didn't taste as good as the one Mother makes, but they did bring me closer to home.

They informed me that Bern now has four big "Bear pits" on the same street where the clock is. Zurich is still the same, though outside the city limits has grown rapidly with new and modernistic homes. However both Bern and Zurich (city proper) have not been changed. Any new homes built within the cities have to follow the old home style and pattern.

I would appreciate it greatly if you could send me……etc.

I am so glad you enjoyed the birthday card as it took me several days to draw it. I never could draw a straight line, so you can imagine how long it took me.

The "Hello Charley" sticker of 1944 certainly brought back memories, the very pleasant ones too. I often wonder if I'll ever return to the company. At the present time, I have so many post-war plans that I couldn't possibly become a Master at any. However, I'll come home first and then we'll see what happens. Yes, my darlings, it will be grand to come home again and be with you but for the present I'm enjoying it to the fullest, wide eyed and all.

Sorry I haven't done too well on this letter. Words seem to fail me and news isn't too interesting at the present time. I'll try again soon.

Remember, I love you and I'll be home someday – a little more experienced in life, a little more understanding, helpful and capable. However, deep down inside I'll be just "Ginny" the little girl who grew up to love and respect her family. All I am to this day I owe to you both, and sincerely want to live up to your expectations of me. I am so very proud of my family, honestly.

Good night and pleasant dreams. Affectionately, Ginny

***"Somewhere in Egypt"***
***10 August 1944***

At this time, I am asking you to join me in my new adventures. If not in person, at least by pen.

You and I have left the hotel and have decided to traverse the city. Neither of us know the streets very well, but feel assured familiar surroundings will direct us toward home eventually. We suddenly notice a Wog squatting on the sidewalk. To our surprise, we noticed people don't really sit; they actually squat. Truly a most awkward, uncomfortable position. At any rate it's their way of relaxing. So let us continue our little journey – a journey through a town in Egypt.

As in any other city on the face of this earth, people pass each other rapidly; each individual having his or her destination in mind. All is well until a Wog practically throws you off balance. "Hey there, what's the big idea anyway. One more knock like that and I bust you wide open." No, it's not a pleasant refined thought, but a human one. You ponder and wonder just why he hit you and finally receive the answer from a reliable source. "Why, my dear ladies, that's the way the Egyptians get their pickups. If you turn around and smile, you are giving them the high sign to show you the way to their rooms. If you are not interested, just keep on walking and pay no attention to them. They'll try somewhere else."

Let's ride a streetcar or as they say a "traem." We can travel quite far for 2 Piastres or 8 cents. Just overlook the fact that there are bugs present. They want a lift too, you know. I really wouldn't mind riding in these things if I could view the scenery, unattractive as it may be. However, staring at a white nightgown tossing wildly before me in the wind is not my conception of beauty. These Wogs don't really have to hang on the outside of the cars. There's always another car.

It's getting rather late and since there is a black-out each evening, let's visit our little "beer parlor" and discuss the events of our day. It's lovely here. Just two rooms. One includes the bar with cokes, beer, etc. and the other WAC necessities and the other has tables painted black and red with cute candles adorning the room. Pictures of WAC's, celebrities and of course men, "God's gift to the feminine world," create THAT atmosphere. It's a place to sit, visit and relax, listen to the girls heart throbs and woes, in our own company PX.

Now, let's reminisce. Remember the sights we saw while riding past the canal? Wogs wash their camels, then their vegetables in the same water and last their own bodies. Then we wonder and are amazed when the health statistics reports state high percentages of diseases. From the canal they make their daily trip into the heart of the city to sell their wares. It is not unusual to see a Wog carrying a huge basket of camel's eyes on his head.

Then too, we have the WOG who realizes the value of important, beautiful expensive pen and pencil sets. It is unwise, let alone unsafe to carry such articles in one's pockets, for rather than not, the Wogs will attack the owner. However, they usually get more than they bargain for and often discover, cement is not too soft or a comfortable place to lie. I witnessed a brawl Sunday and am very happy to report that we G.I.'s came out on top, however only to meet several more opponents a little later.

When a prisoner is released from a penitentiary, a celebration is planned in his honor. There is usually a parade with a band and his friends following directly behind the music, while the ex-prisoner marches ahead of the procession. A glorified crime would be my interpretation. Capone would be twice the character, were he here.

One must not feel too badly when reading about the "conscientious objector." Here in Egypt, when a man does not want to serve his country, he immediately has one eye removed. Being considered physically unfit for duty, will of course, place him in the 4-F category.

To touch the lighter side of things, this evening I'd like to tell you about our experiences with "latrines" or "bains." One evening as expected, nature called, and so yours truly, in Emilie Post's style book 1944, excused herself to powder her shiny nose. Upon inquiring she discovered a door marked "Bain" and proceeded to enter the room. One look was shocking, but most shocking, there lo and behold were three British Soldiers and one G.I. (Yes I counted them.) Very indignantly I approached the owner of the café and demanded to be shown to the "Women's Bain."

He, quite wide eyed and surprised led me back to the identical place where I viewed an unusual scene a few moments hence.

"This is for men and women both," he explained in broken English. "Go in, go in."

"Oh no!" I said.

"Oh yes," he said.

Well, by that time it was decided better to have a shiny nose. This is Egypt!

Oh, I must inform you of the pleasant evening I had with the Swiss acquaintances I made while being a guest at the Swiss Club party August the first. That evening was quite eventful as we had a marvelous dinner, dancing, and movies at the Red Cross. I even remembered how to waltz the Swiss way (or better yet, daddy's way.) Later on in the week ,I was invited to a Roesti-dinner with chicken at the home of Mr. and Mrs. Klauser. An Albert Graff from Zurich was present and we had a perfect evening discussing home, families, the war, etc. Since then, I have never seen this young man, whose company I enjoy, though he is rather reserved, you know, not quite like our American boys. Can't help but say I take our boys any day. The Swiss like the English take forever to loosen up and act natural. That is, the younger men. I have been invited by a Dr. and Mrs. Tadros and a Dr. and Mrs. Hess for dinner too. Am looking forward to some more pleasant evenings.

I can perceive future jurisprudence in Egypt. A post war civil law training program is now in effect. However, I have great doubts whether this baby would remain. I have been reading with great interest about the forthcoming construction of the Saudi Arabian oil lines. Realize the possibility of such an enterprise.

U S A F I M E means: United States Army Forces in the Middle East.

### Cairo, Egypt
### 19 September 1944

Magdalene and I have just returned from what you would call a short vacation or "rest camp" in Alexandria, Egypt.

If you can recall, I had marked pains on my right side the spring of 1943. Recently these pains have recurred to a more distinct pain and appeared to have spread throughout a larger surface of my body. Being slightly concerned and annoyed at this, I went on sick call and after having been examined was informed that I had neuralgia. Apparently, I am more nervous than I think I am. At any rate, the medical officer suggested a rest. Hence our trip to Alexandria.

We took the train up which is a 4 hour run from Cairo. We traveled first class which cost $4. There were six of us in one compartment. Directly across from me sat a woman (not a lady) who must have weighed all of 250 pounds. Her appearance was horrible and her actions disgusting as she sat cross-legged on the seat and persisted in playing with her toes. Her hair was a mass of black strings and she wore cosmetic much too thickly, let alone evenly. With her was her child, a baby of about 22 months, who couldn't open her eyes because of all the filthy flies sitting there. Her main interest was eating and she certainly indulged in some icky, gooey stuff. When the food fell on the dusty and step beaten floor, she just picked it up with her feet (toes) and then proceeded to eat it. At the same time, she was fanning herself with a pair of old, worn and spotted baby diapers. The scene was so nauseating, that at times I feared I was going to donate my noon mess [lunch.]

Kitty corner from her, or next to me, sat a Wog, dressed rather neatly. He appeared to be in his early fifties. On several occasions, he spoke to her in Arabic and at one time he offered her 10 Piastres (40 cents). Magdalene and I thought perhaps he was trying to proposition her and made no bones about our thoughts. In fact, we spoke rather loudly at times.

After approximately two hours, several occupants of this compartment were added by new arrivals. They did not look much better and so Magdalene and I proceeded to take them apart too. (That is, verbally.) Oh yes, we had a marvelous time being catty, until one spoke to us. Mind you, in perfectly good English. Needless to say how we felt. I turned all the colors of the rainbow, tried to advertise "Pepsodent toothpaste" and tried to remember the rules and regulations in Carnegies book, "How to win friends and influence people." But the damage was already done. Guess I am not too good in promoting good welfare and creating the good neighbor policy. After making a resolution not to tear other people apart, for the sake of saving our own neck, we proceeded to call the

Military Police to escort us to our billet. Magdalene got in the back of the jeep and I sat in the front with the driver. We had just left the railroad station, when she let out a scream. With that I turned around immediately and the M.P. slammed on the brakes. I found myself anywhere but in the front seat and Magdalene was hanging in thin air. A Wog had run up to the jeep and had stolen our baggage, and while doing so, almost managed to take her too. It is stranger than fiction, because we were traveling at a good speed. We can't imagine where he came from in such a hurry. To make a long story short, the M.P. chased him and recaptured our baggage and then delivered us to our billet safely. (Remember, I came for a rest.)

Alexandria is extremely dark since they still have a complete blackout. As far as I am concerned, the city is laid out poorly and not to my liking in the least. The only pleasant thing it has to offer is the beach and the sea. It's inhabitants are a mixture of everything and anything. Wogs are poorer and more treacherous than in Cairo. The fleet was in when I was there and British, French, Greek, and American soldiers filled the streets. It is now Ramadan's time for the Wogs and since they have been fasting since the beginning of the month, they are very wild. To add to this, they spend their time smoking Hashish (a dope weed.) Therefore, we have added worries. Every precaution is taken to prevent a riot among the natives, but if and when the time arrives we will be safe in first aid stations.

Getting back to Alexandria: I spent my mornings and afternoons at the beach and as a result possess a beautiful tan. The evenings, however, were far from being restful. One evening, about 7 P.M., Magdalene and I ate dinner at the Red Cross. Instead of walking home to our billet about 7:45, we thought it safer to take a "Gharry" (A taxi here is definitely much too dangerous without an escort.) So we flagged a "gharry" down and said: "Alatool." The driver was black and a close rival to "Lincoln" in height. He sported a mustache a la the villain in any play and jibber jabbered in Arabic as we rode along the dark streets of Alexandria. The horse went extremely slow and therefore it made it easier for the natives to step in the carriage. As Magdalene kept speaking to me, I suddenly noticed this driver was heading in the wrong direction and was slowly leading the horse to the curb. Before I could mention it to her, he stopped completely and after viewing the countryside and seeing nothing but trees and rocks, I knew something was radically wrong. Without any hesitation I leaped from the Gharry into the street and expected Magdalene to follow me. However, she was too paralyzed at that moment. I then ran behind the carriage and directly behind this maniac with the intention of socking him at the earliest possible moment, for he was trying to get either of us. By this time she came to life and jumped to safety too, which made him turn around. There I was, directly in front of him, only about three feet of solid ground between us. I took to my heels immediately, and only left a cloud of dust. By this time he was rip roaring mad and decided to get us by hook or crook. It was a close race, but we won. We ran for two blocks in complete darkness in a strange area with him close behind us. Finally, we discovered familiar territory and found some G.I.'s He then disappeared and these boys proceeded to take us home. (I didn't sleep well that night.)

Another evening we went to one of their best night clubs. In plain English, it was a dive like our taxi dance places. Really, I was quite embarrassed. Curiosity was the only thing that kept me there until midnight. We were out with three soldiers who had returned from Corsica, so I felt reasonably safe. The place was occupied by the British and Greek soldiers and sailors and a small number of American boys. The women, who entertained during the floor show, also danced with the men during the course of the evening. (If you can call it dancing.) It's really a crime the way they lead the men on. They entertain by belly dances and Egyptian Harem dances. Then they do suggestive types with the men. What a life!

The afternoon we left Alexandria for Cairo, another incident occurred. We flew back in a C-54. However, just as we were about to leave the runway, we almost flew into another bomber. That was the closest I have ever come to death. We were all paralyzed at the thought of crashing. Oh, it was so close.

I am now safe and sound on my little bed and about to retire after a most restful journey. Haven't received a single letter in the last three weeks. Do hope everything is fine overseas. Things are really popping here. Wish I could explain!

All my love. Ginny

***Cairo, Egypt***
***28 October 1944***

The other day I was more than amazed to discover that the Wogs milk their horses. Magdalene and I stood in amazement at the scene. It was rather heartbreaking since a young colt stood nearby and witnessed his breakfast being sold.

Last evening I was scrubbing for inspection today, when I was interrupted by loud clamor or sirens, whistles and screams. I thought the Germans were at my back door. It so happened a laundry caught fire. Some Wog evidently left a hot iron stand on a shirt and as a result the building went up in flames and the mob of people went hysterical. Within a few moments the fire engine came roaring down the Ada Pascha. The firemen made quite an appearance with their blue suits and gold hats. With the building in flames, the crowd in hysterics, as I mentioned before, the firemen came to the rescue. Yes, the heroes of Cairo began to put out the flames with buckets of water. No, I haven't made an error. I said and

I mean buckets. No hose in sight. I watched with great interest and after a few moments decided it wouldn't be another Chicago fire. Hence, I continued with my cleaning.

Romeos are present all over the city. Last evening before scrubbing our rooms, I went to El Gammals for a cup of tea and cake. (To date my tummy is still O.K.) Anyway, within five minutes an Egyptian Doctor approached our table and began talking to us. I listened quite attentively and politely at first, however changed my attitude when he decided he was quite lonesome in his large home without a wife. He and his fifty years suddenly needed companionship and I was the answer to his long search – tra la la la.

Several evenings ago we girls drank beer and ate crackers in our "Milk Bar," which is on the first floor, and had quite a discussion about home. It seems strange to walk through the city and not see a single sign of Christmas. The weather alone throws one off the path. We took turns telling of silly incidents and experiences we had in our youth and how we were brought up. Really, we do have loads of fun together at the hotel. Most of us have stopped running around as we have seen all the night spots and it's much too filthy to feel comfortable. We attend concerts, lectures, movies, etc. but we can't just go around the corner to a drugstore for a coke or ice cream. There aren't any and what there is, is dirty. You take a chance when you enter on your own. Sometimes we do though.

It is late evening now of the 29th and I have just returned from a most pleasant afternoon and evening. Five girls and myself visited the Pyramids and Sphinx again and spent most of our time climbing stones with G.I.'s from C.S.G. and Russia. We had supper at the Red Cross and then saw "Lady In The Dark." Except for the movie, I enjoyed it all. And now it's lights out! Good night and pleasant dreams.
Love. Ginny

***Cairo, Egypt***
***2 November 1944***

Time certainly plays an important part in one's life. Since we have been here in Egypt, 15 girls have been operated on for appendicitis. Two had spinal meningitis, several tonsils removed and two returned to the states. Two more will return because of unexpected happenings at home. One never knows what's next.

I had the opportunity to speak to many boys from Russia and also many Bulgarian ex-prisoners. Mother, daddy and Ruthie, I discovered I haven't suffered a bit. Not really suffered. It was hard and hurt badly but in comparison, I never went through hell. They did. It disgusts me so much to hear people complain, complain about each trivial matter, while others, who have reason to, do not.

No, my dears, I have never regretted going overseas. Oh, we do have our ups and downs, but doesn't everyone everywhere? There is no paradise on earth now. Truthfully, it's rather sickening to see all the filth and suffering day in and day out and it will be nice to return to a place where there is cleanliness, happiness, etc. Home. Germany isn't falling as quickly as we had all expected and with added trouble in Italy, it will probably take longer, not forgetting there is another side too – Japan.

You can tell by this writing that I'm tired. I better get some sleep. I'll write again soon.

All my love. Ginny

***Cairo, Egypt***
***4 November 1944***

This is Ginny reporting again from Egypt with the hope that you are ready and willing to read my epistle.

First of all, I would like to describe the new experimental health village, Babins. This is a governmental project very similar to our Jane Adams scheme; and if it proves to be successful will be carried out through entire Egypt.

A bird's eye view of this little town tells us there are approximately five hundred inhabitants, several rows of brick houses, a school, hospital, and many many acres of farmland. Last but not least, we must include the animals – the Fellaheen's most valuable property.

While walking through this experimental town, one wonders whether these people are aware of the change that has taken place in their lives. The reorganization of their homes, living conditions, food supply and education dare not be too evident or radical a change. Time is the only element which can alter the peoples existence; and perhaps someday if this project proves to be successful, Egypt will be placed on a higher standard of living. I have my doubts, however, whether any of us will be fortunate enough to see it progress, let alone be able to witness a complete revolution of this country, as a change in government is unforeseen and that well know time element would spread far out into another generation.

As mid-afternoon approached, we entered one of the homes, home to them, a barren looking place to us. Obviously, there was no furniture to be seen in the living room nor the bedroom.

Their kitchens are more than a contrast to ours, four walls and a doorway constitute the setup and since chimney's are non-existent, there are no ceilings. Stone hearths in the center of the kitchen establish the cooking room.

The fourth room found in these houses is the animal residence. After some inquiring, we discovered that these natives distrust their neighbors and therefore keep the animals in the same house. Remember how valuable they are to the Fellaheen's.

Twilight brings the sandman rather hurriedly due to the lack of electricity, while dawn wakens our Fellaheen's for another days work in the fields. Since there are no beds to make nor clothes to change, I wonder, just why they awaken and rise so frightfully early.

As twilight neared we visited the hospital. Though the interior was not to my liking, it was apparent that patients do survive and return to their families in good health. The hospital is far from being modern and cleanliness is not a principal object. However, we must realize they have at least made an attempt at progressing medically and again the time element enters.

A midwife is the only attendant at childbirth. Naming the child is quite an interesting and unusual ceremony. Several candles are named and then lighted. The child is named after the candle that burns the longest. Sounds like too many names but can't find a substitute since the people are not Christians. At any rate, I hope I have put the idea across. The child usually is called Mahmoud, Mohammed or Hussein. A lock and key is tied around the child's abdomen to ensure long, happy, and successful living. Among other duties, good luck bracelets are worn around the ankles similar to our prison chains. How they can even lift their feet, let alone walk, amazes me.

Schools are very elementary in this area but again I must say it is a beginning. Reading, writing, and arithmetic are taught.

I consider my little venture as something gained. It was truly an interesting afternoon and evening.

Education in Cyprus has been dominated by political considerations. As a result, not too many are at this day and age well educated. As a result. we have the easy, happy go lucky peasant who lives on his small acre of farmland and delights at watching his sheep, cattle and orange groves – no worries – no cares, but a pleasant smile and a friendly attitude.

Yes, we had a furlough we will never forget; pleasant, educational and restful. I hope the above mentioned paragraphs not only clarified my statement, "Life can be beautiful," "Experience is the only teacher," has become my faithful proverb. For secondary choice I'll take, "a picture is worth a thousand words." Hence, you must see my album when it reaches the States, which should be shortly.

# 9
# Finding Love Again

## Harvey

Harvey Davis was born July 9, 1918 in Watertown, New York to Everett Davis and Elsie Bennett. Harvey had three siblings, Fred, George, and Robert. As a young child, Harvey's father left the family. Elise, now a divorced mother, unable to raise three children on her own, placed two of the boys, Harvey and Fred, into the Jefferson County Orphan Asylum in Watertown before 1930. Elsie took the oldest son George and the youngest Robert and moved to Chicago.[79]

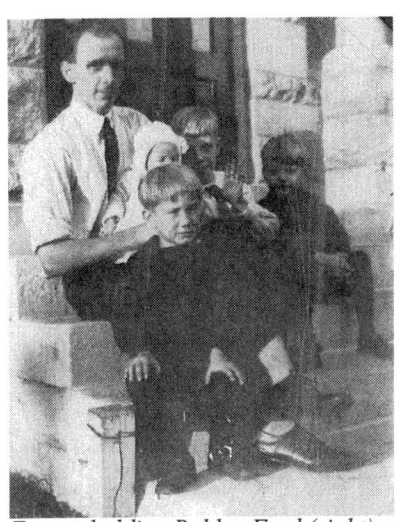

*Everett holding Bobby, Fred (right) Geroge (center), and Harvey (left). Courtesy Virginia S. Davis.*

In the early part of the 20th century, there were many families who used orphanages to place children for short and indefinite periods of time. Single mothers, due to divorce, widowhood, or other circumstances which required them to work, often placed children in orphanages when there was not the option of leaving them with family. Children without parents were placed in these homes until they were adopted or grew to the age of majority. During this time, these orphanages served as a form of public aid to help families. Elsie used this aid to help care for her children even though it meant breaking their hearts.

*Finding Love Again* 119

Harvey and Fred grew up in separate wings of the Orphan Asylum, two hearts joined by blood but separated by distance. Sadly, the two boys barely knew each other as brothers and neither had a real place to call home. At the age of 18, Harvey was ready to be on his own and began working in Watertown. Elsie had married again, this time to Earl Sherrill, and brought her now grown sons, from Watertown to Chicago.[80] Their time together in Chicago would be short lived as the country joined the world war. Both Fred and Harvey joined the Army Air Corps and were sent overseas.

Both Harvey and Fred were stationed in North Africa for a period in 1943. Fred then was transferred to Sicily with the 98th Bomb Group, 344th Bomb Squadron (Heavy). On a bombing raid to Wiener Neustadt in Austria on November 2, 1943, Fred's plane was shot down and he was declared Missing in Action.[81] Harvey was left wondering what happened to his brother.

## Two Hearts Meet

In October 1944, Ginny and Magdalene flew to Devesior for a military weekend dance party. Excitement filled the air as the two friends arrived at the air field. After the plane touched down, Ginny stood, grabbed her Musette bag, and flung it over her left shoulder. She and the other passengers began departing the plane. Coming down the stairs, Ginny held onto the railing with her right hand while her left hand held the Musette bag against her shoulder. As she descended, the bag slipped off her shoulder and started swinging. Ginny was unable to control the bag and hold onto the railing at the same time. By the time she got close to the bottom of the stairs, her bag had swung and hit an

*Harvey Davis in Africa 1943. Courtesy Virginia S. Davis.*

Army Air Corps Sergeant waiting there to greet the WACs, in the face causing him to lose his equilibrium! The man fell to the ground stunned. Who was this soldier Ginny had innocently knocked off his feet? Harvey Davis.

Ginny said, "Harvey was so angry at being hit in the face that he was going to use his French on that ….. until he looked up and saw her legs and then looked up more and saw her concerned expression and melted." Surprisingly, there was no yelling from Harvey. There was only a brief linking of hearts. Ginny, mortified over the debacle, apologized profusely about hitting Harvey and he graciously accepted her apologies. He then asked her on a date. He said to her, "That's the least you can do after injuring me."[82] That date lasted 58 years.

## A Chance Encounter and Resolution

After the weekend was over, Ginny and Magdalene returned to their base and Ginny did not see Harvey for several weeks. War life for both resumed as usual in their separate bases. On November 12, 1944, Ginny decided to walk after work, in the dark, to the U.S. O. Building for a break. Her heart yearned for peace and she had been so homesick for her family, she ignored the warnings against walking alone after dark. Ginny walked and walked and ended up outside the U.S.O. Building where there was a bus stop. Ginny said, "For some reason I was being protected."[83] Suddenly she heard someone scream, "Ginny……Ginny."

Turning, she saw a thin man in uniform standing there. Focusing in the dark, she realized the man was Harvey! He explained to her had been battling Bacillary Dysentery in the hospital and had lost a lot of weight. Excited to be reunited, the couple went out for a Coke and talked. As they sat down on a brick wall to talk, Harvey laid out his handkerchief and spread it down so Ginny could sit on it and not damage or soil her uniform. What a true gentleman.

The gentleman was determined not to let weeks go by before he saw the woman who had captured his heart. What he did not realize was she would provide the answer to a year-long mystery.

Just prior to November 20, Ginny and Harvey had their third date. That day, while working in the Medical Dispensary Records Department, Ginny received a Battle Casualty Report for a Fred A. Davis, serial no. O-683416. The War Department had issued a Finding of Death (FOD) on this soldier.[84] This meant Fred had been Missing in Action for a year and the War Department had declared him legally deceased. It was Ginny's job to look up Fred's personnel information so the family could be notified of the Finding of Death.

Ginny knew Harvey had a brother named Fred who was in the Army Air Corps, but was unsure if this was the correct man. She wrote Fred's serial number down and took it to dinner with her. Near the end of dinner, Ginny quietly asked Harvey if he knew his brother's serial number. Harvey replied, "Yes." He pulled it out of his wallet and read it to Ginny. Sadly, Ginny had to inform Harvey that his brother had been killed.

> During World War II, information was transferred by telephone via wires set up by the soldiers as they moved from place to place. It was also sent by mail which was transported as the troops moved by land or sea. The communication was very slow in many cases because of the continual movement of the front lines. When a person was missing or killed in action, it was not always reported immediately because of the location. In those days, there was no internet, cell phone, television, or radio that transmitted information immediately.
>
> Communication only went to the next-of-kin so Harvey would not have known about his brother until a letter arrived from Fred's wife or their mother that he had been killed. It was serendipity that Ginny received this notice.
>
> Today, through records, we know that Fred had been flying over Austria and was shot down behind enemy lines. He was killed on November 2, 1943, but was initially reported Missing in Action. The Chicago Tribune reported this status on Christmas Day 1943.[85] His death was confirmed in November 1944. His wife Patricia was notified of his death in late November and the Chicago Tribune reported it in the newspaper on November 23, 1944.[86]

# 10

# Harvey and Ginny's Courtship

By early December, Harvey had been transferred from his base to Payne Field outside of Cairo where Ginny was living and working. This change allowed the two to spend more time together for the duration of the war. The couple spent Christmas Eve at Kurstaal Restaurant which was a short walk from the WAC billet. Ginny and Harvey enjoyed dinner and dancing until curfew. Many days were spent together after work hours and New Year's Eve was spent dining and dancing as the couple welcomed in the New Year. Hearts connected and love blossomed even during wartime. The change in Ginny was evident in her next letter home as love seeped from every word.

*Cairo, Egypt*
*January 1945*

I am certain that after reading this letter you will doubt whether there have been any moments of regrets since I have been overseas, and whether I have been satisfied. So here is my report about my furlough, at the Isle of Cyprus.

Cyprus, often described by poets as Love's Island, by Empire critics as a Cinderella, and by apologetic proconsuls as an unfortunate exception to an otherwise golden rule, is an interesting island. It was there where I enjoyed a most heavenly out-of-this-world furlough.

Cyprus is situated about 40 miles from the coast of Asia Minor to the North and about 60 miles from Syria to the East. It is the third largest island in the Mediterranean, the largest being Sicily and Sardinia. It has an area of 3,584 square miles, being 140 miles from long from east to west, and 60 miles from north to south. From my bedroom window I could see the coast of Turkey.

The beauty of this island is difficult to describe, for few words could possibly delineate its scenic views of statuesque mountains, flowing streams, colorful fruit trees and playful sheep along the coast of the deep blue sea of the Mediterranean. Serenity personified.

Harvey and I departed from Cairo during the holiday season, with the intention of spending both the old and the new year on this little island. Our trip was more than delightful since we flew in the General's personal plane and were able to relax in soft green cushioned seats. The trip took two hours and in that period of time, the desert land had been left far behind and the approaching of mountainous terrain was more than a welcome sight.

We and the other military travelers stayed at the Dome Hotel, which is patterned after a lovely Swiss chalet and is situated along the seashore with the mountains in the background. This resort presented a picture of friendliness, cleanliness and quietness. Many a time, I could hardly understand that it was I who was enjoying such a visit during the hours of world turmoil. It almost seemed like the chapters of two different stories had become mixed.

My room, #39, was a soft cream and blue combination with an open fireplace and a terrace facing the coast of Turkey. Harvey bunked with Colonel Bill Carson in room #36. Meals were served at 10:00 a.m. and 1:00 and 8:00 p.m. with tea in the sitting room between 4:00 and 5:00. I gained four pounds, so I am certain that alone speaks well for the meal situation.

Our first afternoon found us strolling along the seashore, enjoying the fresh salt air and watching the high waves splashing over the breakers, while the dark clouds above clung closely to the earth, hovering maliciously over the mountains. The few drops of rain soon turned into a downpour and so yours truly and company sought refuge in a nearby fort, Fort of Cherimes. It was then and there I learned the history of Cyprus, which is truly an interesting one.

First of all, Cyprus is the only British possession which serves to illustrate the history of activities of the Greeks. Alongside the sad story of neglect and antiquities in the distant past, crawls the present day picture of a country lost in the conservative way of life and almost entirely untouched by the progress which has taken place in recent years on the mainland. It opens with the fantastic stories of mythology. The wider world which now shares the state of education is less credulous. History, and with it mythology, is being "debunked."

Modern reaction to all these stories of pagan gods and goddesses, who played hide and seek with our imagination as well as with their own elusive beings, runs in different directions. Some of us may feel twinges of pity for these unfortunate deities who were condemned to sport and to woo in a state of nature amidst the thorny bushes and plants with which the island is carpeted. The goddess of love, the Astarts of the Phoenicians, the Aphrodite of the Greeks, the Venus of the Romans is said to have had her miraculous birth in Cyprus, rising mature and splendid from the sea foam, washing the coast of Paphos.

The first Greek settlement was bout 2,000 – 1,500 BC and with it arose the great conflict between the Phoenicians. The old Fort we entered stood as a protector for centuries, while battles were fought between the Greeks and Phoenicians and Turks. Turks and Romans, and the English. To this day, the old Fort stands aged and war torn, but faces boldly the prospects of another conflict.

Cyprus, they told us, became a Roman Province, administered by Cicero. It was later given to Egypt by Julius Caesar, and then Mark Anthony presented it to Cleopatra.

When the advent of Christianity shook the world, Cyprus was firmly in the hands of Rome. We were informed that there were already in the island populous settlements of Jews, who had fled there owing to disturbances in the Holy Land. These were the first to be converted by the wave of Christian refugees who came to Cyprus. In 117 AD, the Jews of Cyprus revolted against the Romans and as a result were expelled from the island. To this day one can see or feel considerable antipathy towards the Jews by the Cypriots.

With all this in mind, we returned to our hotel and had tea in the sitting room.

The Hotel is Greek owned, but most of the people we met were British. I was fortunate in meeting an English colonel who had a chauffeur and car, and offered his kind services as a guide for the duration of our stay. He, Col. Campbell, introduced Harvey and me to Mr. Redway, the island's governor; Mr. Simpson, an old retired English Colonel, and Mr. and Mrs. Collver, the owners of the Cyprus Power and Light Company, originally from Australia. From our second day on we were entertained royally by the "Elites" of Love's island with dinners, dances, teas, etc. The sun rose and set on we, two Americans.

New Year's Eve was spent spreading good cheer among the people. I danced with the English, The Greek, the Turk, Egyptian, Australian, Polish, Italian, and American representatives and refugees – a conglomeration of nationalities, if I ever saw any.

The morning of the third found two Americans hiking up the mountain side with the St. Hilarion as their goal. Time of departure was exactly 10:45 a.m. Time of return 7:30 p.m. the 8 hours 45 minutes proved to be most delightful, awe-inspiring, yet tiring. The scenery was gorgeous, the weather perfect, and the company unsurpassable, and so I most naturally had a marvelous time. However, the higher the altitude, the harder the breathing, and many times I thought my strength would give way. It was mind over matter. I was determined to reach the top, 3,452 feet, and I did.

Once there, we saw the castle which existed prior to the arrival of Richard the Lionhearted and the subsequent era. From the queen's window I could view the entire north eastern part of the Island. The adjacent mountains seemed to loom low and dark against the red fires of the sunset and the forest of firs and stately cedars attracted my eyes. Baby sheep followed their guides along the winding trails, over the rocks and flowing streams of cool mountain water. The faint whistle of the wind against the aged rocks of the castle of many wars was the only sound. The strangest feeling of experiencing a few moments of complete quietness far above in the spacious skies cannot be related to you; for it seemed as if I were in another world.

The trip down was far more convenient, for I rode a donkey. Harvey and the others had to walk.

The following day we rode bicycles to the nearby villages; nearby being 20 miles. We ate at the peasants homes and were amazed at their kind and friendly hospitality.

The colonel took us sightseeing several times and we visited the historical places along the eastern coast. We visited Famagusta, the well-known ship building center, and the city of Salamis. They are excavating the latter now. In fact, I dug up a carved marble stone which was estimated as being approximately 1,000 years old. It will make a beautiful ring when set.

I could go into lengthy detail about Famagusta and Salamis, but time will not permit. So I will merely mention that both cities are extremely wealthy in antiquities.

We spent some time in Nicosia, the capital of Cyprus, the city of all cities. Most of the cathedrals there were built during the "Golden Age" 1192-1489 and proved to be most interesting.

After King Richard sold the island, the Venetians took over and the Cypriot life of culture confined itself to maintenance of order. Then in 1571-1878, the Turks took over and the people enjoyed a spiritual respite. In 1878, it became a British subject. So you see Cyprus has been in so many different hands that no one knows very much about what places of antiquity belong to which age.

The only thing I found evident was that every Cypriot claims to be a Greek. (There is food for thought.) Remember,

## 128 *Harvey and Ginny's Courtship*

Cypriots had not been consulted when they found themselves suddenly transferred as part of a bargain, from one alien ruler to another and indeed, it must have been difficult to show their loyalty to the Powers that protected their Minority Rights. Education in Cyprus has been dominated by political considerations. As a result, not too many are at this day and age well educated. As a result, we have the easy, happy go lucky peasant who lives on his small acre of farmland and delights at watching his sheep, cattle and orange groves – no worries – no cares, but a pleasant smile and a friendly attitude.

*Harvey and Ginny in Cyprus.*

Yes, we had a furlough we will never forget; pleasant, educational and restful. I hope the above mentioned paragraphs not only clarified my statement, "Life can be beautiful," "Experience is the only teacher," has become my faithful proverb. For secondary choice I'll take, "a picture is worth a thousand words." Hence, you must see my album when it reaches the States, which should be shortly.

## The Duration of the War

On May 8, 1945, the war in Europe officially ended. Although the fighting had ended, the job of recovery of missing and wounded soldiers and the removal of troops had just begun. Ginny spent the duration of the war in Cairo, continuing her work in the Medical Dispensary, and spending time with Harvey when time allowed. She and Harvey traveled to the Pyramids and spent many hours exploring the ancient history and deepening their relationship.

On May 18, 1945, Ginny and the Cairo Detachment of WACs and other soldiers were sent to Camp Huckstep to celebrate the 3rd anniversary of the founding of the WAC. Harvey was able to accompany Ginny to the celebration where they picnicked, played sports games and listened to speeches. Toward the end of the day, a torrential downpour hit and everyone had to run for cover at the base hospital. When it ended, the WACs were taken back to Cairo and the men returned to their base at Payne Field. Ginny reported in her memoir that Payne Field was a 'seaplane' base for a while during the downpour, the field had flooded.

*Harvey and Ginny.*

Due to the rainy conditions at Payne Field and the number of years the men had been overseas, the military chose to close the base and send the men back to the States for reassignment. Harvey left Egypt several months before Ginny. When Harvey arrived in Chicago he went to visit Ginny's parents and sister. The two had already notified Ginny's family that they planned to be married after the war.

With the war in Europe over, the military awaited victory in the Pacific. It finally arrived on August 15, 1945, now known as Victory in Japan (V-J Day.) Now it was a wait and see game as to how quickly the Army would tabulate points for service and begin discharging troops.

By Early September, Ginny began having pains on her right side. Years earlier she had her appendix removed. This was her second trip to the base hospital for treatment and doctors said fresh milk was the cure. Unfortunately, there was none to be had in Cairo and the military decided to send Ginny back to the States to recover.

On September 24, 1945, Ginny flew from Cairo to Coral Gables, Florida. Ginny was billeted in the Biltmore Hotel where many returning and recuperating veterans were stationed. Her diet consisted of milk, milk, and more milk. After a few weeks she was cured. And the best part, Harvey was there to greet her!

Harvey was stationed nearby and was able to visit Ginny two to three times a week. The two bought wedding rings, planned their wedding, and spent time on the pier watching the waves ebb in and out.

On November 1, 1945, Harvey was flown to Patterson Field in Ohio and received his Honorable Discharge from the Army Air Corps. A few weeks later on November 24, Ginny was flown to Fort Des Moines, Iowa and Honorably Discharged. The two were now free to finish planning their wedding and start a new chapter of their lives.

A quiet ceremony consisting of family and close friends was held on December 9, 1945 at 8:00 p.m. at the Presbyterian Church in Chicago. Reverend William Jones officiated. This marked the beginning of a new life for Ginny and Harvey. Two hearts joined for 58 years on earth and forever after death. Together they raised two beautiful children, a daughter and son.

Ginny and Harvey's family grew over those 58 years to include (at the time of this writing,) five grandchildren, 5 great grandchildren, and two great, great grandchildren. Their life together on earth ended when Harvey died of colon cancer on December 22, 2002. To cope with the loss of her husband, Ginny hand-wrote several large volumes of her life's history. Copies were given to all of her descendants. Through this act and many others, Ginny spread her knowledge, patience, and love to everyone she met.

*Harvey and Ginny Davis, October 2002.*

# 11
# Five Hearts Connected

Ginny's story is more than one woman's survival after tragedy and how she coped by serving her country in a time when the roles of women and the world dramatically changed. It is a story of love and loss, and how life and death connect us all through time. It is about serendipitous moments when the universe places someone or something in your path that changes your life forever.

When I started researching my family's history in 1996, I had no idea where to find Ginny. No one in the family knew. She and Bob had been married only three weeks. Through my research, I found the Flying Tigers Association and posted a query about Bob on their message board. It took nine years before I got the response I was never expecting. Ginny's grandson had seen my post and Ginny emailed mein December 2005. The email set off a series of events that were unimaginable to me at the time.

Ginny sent me letters detailing her life with Robert, photos of the two of them together and of his life with the Flying Tigers in China. She also had a copy of his Flying Tiger war diary. It was incredible to read about a man I barely knew and began to understand and feel the love the two shared. Two hearts connected.

I put all of Bob's materials and Ginny's letters away and we lost touch until 2010. That year was the beginning of a very difficult time for me personally. It was also the year I started my research business and decided to write Bob's story. He deserved to be remembered and Ginny approved wholeheartedly. Bob's story, To Soar with the Tigers, was released in 2011. Through this book, their hearts had connected with mine in a bond that can never be broken.

In April 2012, just after her 90th birthday, I visited and met Ginny for the first time. My life was falling apart and my heart was shattered. When I arrived on her doorstep we hugged and giggled like 16 year old school girls. Two hearts joined. We spent two and a half days talking, sharing stories, shedding only a few tears, and laughing a lot! If anyone had seen us they would have thought we were giggly teenagers. Ginny shared the many volumes of family history she wrote – hand wrote not typed – in thick binders. I read the full story of her life with Bob and what followed after his death. Ginny shared an incredible story with me about her time in the WAC in Egypt where she met her second husband Harvey. We shared personal stories of difficult times in our lives and seemed to bring each other some peace. The air crackled with happiness and love. Four hearts connected.

During that visit, Ginny and I talked about why it had not occurred to us before April 2012 to meet. We both agreed that everything happens when it is supposed to and for the reason it is supposed to. Perhaps we were not supposed to meet until that moment, a moment when I really needed guidance and love from someone very wise whose heart was full of love.

When the visit ended, I left for home feeling more confident about some decisions I had made and so blessed to have had the opportunity to spend time with this incredible woman. It is a moment in time I will never forget.

In late 2012, I began writing a book about my military ancestors who died in World War II. I felt a deep need to ensure these men, who were never able to return to tell their stories, were never forgotten. They say you die twice, the first time when you physically die and the second when someone utters your name for the last time. I did not want that to happen to these men.

Writing my military ancestor book made me think again of Ginny's story. She is such an incredible, strong, loving person who survived a great deal of tragedy at a young age. She took that grief and turned it into a new direction by taking up Robert's fight and serving in the Armed Forces during World War II. There was more to her story than one act of choosing not to let tragedy define the rest of your life.

Ginny told me repeatedly, 'I never did anything.' Or, 'what I did was not as important as what the fighting men did.' Her service, however, laid the foundation for women to serve and bear arms in the future. Her service and that of women in all branches, helped lay a greater foundation for women to have the option to work outside the home and follow their dreams. Because of women like Ginny who served in World War II as part of the war or at home, I have the option to follow my dreams and live the life of which I dream. It is to Ginny and other women from her generation that I say thank you. Thank you for your service and the life you enabled me to live. I will forever be grateful.

This is what her story needed to convey. However, when I approached her about writing her story, she responded again with, 'I never did anything.' When I explained it was a story of loss and moving on, she agreed.

I visited Ginny again in July 2013 and spent four days pouring over her scrapbooks, photographs, and records. I recorded interviews and discovered pieces of her story she didn't know or had not thought about in years. One piece was what happened to Harvey's brother Fred during the war. It was as if Fred was asking to not be forgotten as I located puzzle piece after puzzle piece about his life and death. What Ginny and I did not realize at the time was that Fred's story would play a role in my future through military research and writing. Five hearts connected.

Virginia's story gives us hope after loss. It demonstrates the promise of a new life and love. Hers is the fulfillment of a destiny that spanned more than 70 years reaching into the present day. Her story connects us to the past and teaches life lessons in the present, all done through love. We are shown life goes on after death.

When you get right down to it, the main purpose in our lives is to love. Giving and receiving love is what Ginny has done her entire life. She raised and supported a family with Harvey and in 2002 lost him to cancer. Once again she loved and lost. Yet today, she will tell you, "I miss him [Harvey] terribly. Memories are wonderful, but loneliness equals sadness. Thank God for family, friends, and many acquaintances, life **DOES** go on, until we too are called home.

# Endnotes

1. Ancestry.com, Cook County, Illinois, Birth Certificates Index, 1871-1922 (Online publication - Provo, UT, USA: Ancestry.com Operations, Inc., 2011.Original data - "Illinois, Cook County Birth Certificates, 1878–1922." Index. FamilySearch, Salt Lake City, Utah, 2009. Illinois. Cook County Birth Certificates, 1878–1922. Illinois D), Ancestry.com, http://www.Ancestry.com.

2. Illinois, Department of Public Health, Birth Certificates, certificate no. 60349, Ruth Viola Scharer, 1925; Illinois Department of Public Health, Springfield, IL.

3. Hawthorne Works Museum, Hello Charley 1963, pamphlet (Cicero, IL. : 1963), inside panel 2.

4. Davis, Ginny. "Interview with Ginny Davis." Personal interview. 19 July 2013.

5. "New York Passenger Lists, Roll T715_99: 1820-1957." Database Ancestry.com. (http://www.ancestry.com : accessed 5 May 2010), entry for Peter Brouk, age 11, arrived New York, New York, 1900 [Noordland].

6. Florida Office of Vital Statistics, death certificate 23196 (1942), Robert R. Brouk; Bureau of Vital Records, Tallahassee.

7. "Social Security Death Index." Database Ancestry.com (http://www.ancestry.com : accessed 25 September 2010), entry for Harold Brouk, 1983, SS no. 336-18-0271.

8. City of Chicago, Illinois, probate case files, no. 43P 1805, Robert R. Brouk (1943), Petition for Letters of Administration, 12 March 1943; Circuit Clerk's Office, Chicago.

9. "1910 United States Federal Census Roll T624_254 : 1910." Database Ancestry.com. (http://www.ancestry.com : accessed 3 September 2010), entry for Peter Brouk, Chicago, Illinois.

10. "Richard Kauffman Heads Cicero Business Group," Chicago Daily Tribune (Chicago), 8 March 1931, p. H5; digital images, ProQuest (http://www.proquest.umi.com : accessed 3 June 2010), Historical Newspaper Collection.

11. "J. Sterling Morton Year Book 1935." Database Ancestry.com. (http://www.ancestry.com : accessed 1 May 2010), entry for Robert Brouk, Cicero, Illinois.

12. Karen Halla, Cicero, Illinois. [(E-address for private use),] to Jennifer Holik, email, 10 May 2010, "Re: Historical Society of Cicero," Robert Brouk Correspondence File, Robert Brouk Book Research Files; privately held by Jennifer Holik [(E-address) & street address for private use,] Woodridge, Illinois.

13. "Wrestlers Have Largest Squad For Many Years," (Cicero) Morton Collegian, 6 November 1936, p. 4, col. 4.

14. "Cicero Chapter of Builders to Induct Leaders," Chicago Daily Tribune (Chicago), 21 June 1936, p. W7; digital images, ProQuest (http://www.proquest.umi.com : accessed 3 June 2010), Historical Newspaper Collection.

15. Wrestling Club, column and photograph, in Pioneer Yearbook. ca. 1937, p. 66;. Held by Morton Junior College Library, [3801 S. Central Avenue,] Cicero, Illinois, 1937.

16. "Class Prophecy," (Cicero) Morton Collegian, 28 May 1937, p. 2, col. 4.

17. Robert Brouk sophomore photograph, in Pioneer Yearbook, ca. 1937, pg 91; Held by Morton Junior College Library, [3801 S. Central Avenue,] Cicero, Illinois, 1937.

18. "Untitled," (Berwyn) Berwyn Life, 11 November 1942, p. 1, cols. 4-5.

19. "Nine Young Chicagoans Receive Commissions as Lieutenants in Army Air Corps Reserve :Fifth Recent Class. " Chicago Daily Tribune (Chicago), 31 August 1940, p. 6; digital images, ProQuest (http://www.proquest.umi.com : accessed 3 June 2010), Historical Newspaper Collection.

20. "Tiger Diary," (Chicago) Herald-American, 26 July 1942, p. 1.

21. "Cicero to Honor Own Flying Tiger: Day of Tribute to all Fighters is Next Sunday." Chicago Daily Tribune (Chicago), 26 July 1942, p. W1; digital images, ProQuest (http://www.proquest.umi.com : accessed 3 June 2010), Historical Newspaper Collection.

22. Virginia S. Davis (Phoenix, Arizona) to "Dear Jen", letter, 1 February 2006; information on Robert Brouk; Robert Brouk Correspondence File; Robert Brouk Book Research Files; privately held by Jennifer Holik, [address held for private use] Woodridge, Illinois, 2006.

23. Virginia S. Davis to "Dear Jen," 1 February 2006.

24. "It's Bob Brouk Day Today," (Berwyn) Berwyn Life, 2 August 1942, p. 1, col. 5.

25. "Huge Turnout Predicted for Brouk Fete Sunday," (Berwyn) Berwyn Life, 31 July 1942, p. 3, col. 1.

26. "Capt. Bob Brouk," (Berwyn) Berwyn Life, 14 October 1942, p. 10, col. 7.

27. War Department Report of Death 29 December 1942; Individual Deceased Personnel File; Military Textual Reference Branch, National Archives, College Park, MD.

28. Compiled Army Air Force Accident Report, Robert R. Brouk, Captain, 50th Fighter Group, 10th Fighter Squadron, Records of the Army Air Force, p. 20.

29. Virginia S. Davis (Brouk), "Memoir 1918 – 2010" (MS, Phoenix, Arizona, 2010), p. 139; privately held by Virginia S. Davis, [Address for private use,] Phoenix, Arizona, 2010.

30. "Flying Tiger's bride-to-be gets license," (Chicago) The Daily Times, Chicago, 25 December 1942, p. 20, col. 3.

31. Virginia S. Davis (Scharer), "Memoir 1918 – 2010," 145.

32. Virginia S. Davis (Scharer), "Memoir 1918 – 2010," 154.

33. Virginia S. Davis (Scharer), "Memoir 1918 – 2010," 155.

34. Military Service Publishing Company. The Officer's Guide. Harrisburg: The Military Service Publishing Company, 54.

35. Treadwell, Mattie E. U.S. Army in World War II Special Studies. The Women's Army Corps. Washington, D.C., Office of the Chief of Military History. Department of the Army: 1954, p.5.

36. Treadwell, Mattie E. U.S. Army in World War II Special Studies. The Women's Army Corps. Washington, D.C., Office of the Chief of Military History. Department of the Army: 1954, p.10-11.

37. Military Service Publishing Company. The Officer's Guide. Harrisburg: The Military Service Publishing Company, 59-60.

38. Military Service Publishing Company. The Officer's Guide. Harrisburg: The Military Service Publishing Company, 61.

39. Treadwell, Mattie E. U.S. Army in World War II Special Studies. The Women's Army Corps. Washington, D.C., Office of the Chief of Military History. Department of the Army: 1954, p.16-17.

40. Treadwell, Mattie E. U.S. Army in World War II Special Studies. The Women's Army Corps. Washington, D.C., Office of the Chief of Military History. Department of the Army: 1954, p.19.

41. "WAAC Mobilization Day Scheduled for Tomorrow," (Cicero) Cicero Life, 9 April 1943, p. 1, col. 4.

42. Memoir pg. 157 news article "Listener's Choice."

43. Special Orders No. 107 dated 4 May 1943, Chicago, Illinois. Headquarters Sixth Service Command Army Service Forces. Record Group 160; National Archives and Records Administration, Washington, D.C.

44. Memoir pg. 159 news article "Fort Oglethorpe's 13,000th Waac Is the Widow of a Flying Tiger."

45. Miller, Grace Porter. Call of Duty A Montana Girl in World War II. (Baton Rouge: Louisiana State Press, 1999,) 6-7.

46. Memoir pg. 159 notes next to photographs.

47. Special Orders No. 191 dated 22 Jul 1943, Fort Oglethorpe, Georgia.

48. "Spotlight on: Ginny Davis," Red Hat Mommas of Pinnacle Peak (November 2005).

49. Davis, Virginia, "This Could Be My Job" radio transcript, 1943. Privately held by Virginia Davis.

50. Virginia S. Davis (Phoenix, Arizona) to "Dear Jen", letter, 1 February 2006; information on Robert Brouk; Robert Brouk Correspondence File; Robert Brouk Book Research Files; privately held by Jennifer Holik, [address held for private use] Woodridge, Illinois, 2006.

51. Davis, Virginia. "Press Release, undated, Women's Army Corp official part of Army." Privately held by Virginia Davis.

52. Davis, Virginia. "Untitled," radio transcript, 1943. Privately held by Virginia Davis.

53. Memoir page 166, letter to Western Electric dated September 2, 1943, except in The Microphone Newsletter.

54. Davis, Virginia. "Radio Broadcast Saturday, September 25, 1943" radio transcript, 1943. Privately held by Virginia Davis.

55. Davis, Virginia. "Radio Broadcast Saturday, October 2, 1943" radio transcript, 1943. Privately held by Virginia Davis.

56. Virginia S. Davis (Scharer), "Memoir 1918 – 2010," 173.

57. Virginia S. Davis (Scharer), "Memoir 1918 – 2010, Mission for Tonight newspaper clipping," 176.

58. Davis, Virginia. "Sub-station Weekly Report, January 4, 1944." Privately held by Virginia Davis.

59. Davis, Virginia. "Memoir page 178, answer to transfer request," 11 Feb 1944. Privately held by Virginia Davis.

60. Davis, Virginia. "Memoir page 179, answer to transfer request," 11 Feb 1944. Privately held by Virginia Davis.

61. Starbird, Ethel A. When Women First Wore Army Shoes, (New York: I Universe, Inc.,) 44.

62. Virginia S. Davis (Scharer), "Memoir 1918 – 2010," 186.

63. http://www.488thportbattalion.org/The_Santa_Rosa.html The US Army Transport, Santa Rosa page.

64. Virginia S. Davis (Scharer), "Memoir 1918 – 2010," 186.

65. Virginia S. Davis (Scharer), "Memoir 1918 – 2010," 187-188.

66. Virginia S. Davis (Scharer), "Memoir 1918 – 2010," 189-191.

67. Virginia S. Davis (Scharer), "Memoir 1918 – 2010," 192.

68. Virginia S. Davis (Scharer), "War scrapbook letter collection."

69. Virginia S. Davis (Scharer), "Memoir 1918 – 2010," 193.

70. Virginia S. Davis (Scharer), "Memoir 1918 – 2010," 194.

71. Virginia S. Davis (Scharer), "Memoir 1918 – 2010," 195.

72. Virginia S. Davis (Scharer), "Memoir 1918 – 2010," 196.

73. Virginia S. Davis (Scharer), "Memoir 1918 – 2010," 197.

74. Virginia S. Davis (Scharer), "Memoir 1918 – 2010," 197-198.

75. Virginia S. Davis (Scharer), "Memoir 1918 – 2010," 201.

76. Virginia S. Davis (Scharer), "Memoir 1918 – 2010," 202-203.

77. Virginia S. Davis (Scharer), "Memoir 1918 – 2010," 204.

78. National Cemetery Administration. U.S. Veterans Gravesites, ca.1775-2006 [database on-line]. Provo, UT, USA: Ancestry.com Operations Inc, 2006.

79. Year: 1930; Census Place: Watertown, Jefferson, New York; Roll: 1443; Page: 14A; Enumeration District: 0055; Image: 904.0; FHL microfilm: 2341178.

80. Year: 1940; Census Place: Chicago, Cook, Illinois; Roll: T627_956; Page: 14B; Enumeration District: 103-1153.

81. Missing Air Crew Reports (MACRs) of the U.S. Army Air Forces, 1942-1947, MACR 42-9957, 2 Nov 1943, Frederick Allen Davis O-683416.

82. Davis, Ginny. "Interview with Ginny Davis." Personal interview. 19 July 2013.

83. Davis, Ginny. "Interview with Ginny Davis." Personal interview. 19 July 2013.

84. War Department Battle Casualty Report for Fred A. Davis, O-683416, 20 Nov. 1944. National Archives, College Park, MD.

85. Soldiers who are missing in action. 1943. Chicago Daily Tribune (1923-1963), Dec 25, 1943. http://search.proquest.com/docview/176900590?accountid=38403 (accessed October 24, 2013).

86. CHICAGO AIRMEN DIE IN ACTION; 1 MAN MISSING. 1944. Chicago Daily Tribune (1923-1963), Nov 23, 1944. http://search.proquest.com/docview/177042576?accountid=38403 (accessed October 24, 2013).

87. Virginia S. Davis (Scharer), "Memoir 1918 – 2010," 262.

88. Virginia S. Davis (Scharer), "Memoir 1918 – 2010," 263.

89. Davis, Ginny. "Letter regarding service from Ginny Davis." Letter. 30 July 2013, p. 3.

# Bibliography

Ayling, Keith. Calling All Women. New York: Harper and Brothers Publishers, 1942.

Bugbee, Sylvia J. editor. An Officer and a Lady. Hanover: University Press of New England, 2004.

Davis, Virginia. "This Could Be My Job" radio transcript, 1943. Privately held by Virginia Davis.

Davis, Virginia. "Press Release, undated, Women's Army Corp official part of Army." Privately held by Virginia Davis.

Davis, Virginia. "Radio Broadcast Saturday, October 2, 1943" radio transcript, 1943. Privately held by Virginia Davis.

Davis, Virginia. "Sub-station Weekly Report, January 4, 1944." Privately held by Virginia Davis.

Davis, Virginia. "Untitled," radio transcript, 1943. Privately held by Virginia Davis.

Herman, Cpl. Vic. Winnie the WAC. Philadelphia: David McKay Company, 1945.

Larson, C. Kay. 'Til I Come Marching Home. A Brief History of American Women in World War II. Pasadena, MD: The Minerva Center, 1995.

Lorentzen, Lois Ann, and Turpin, Jennifer, editors. The Women & War Reader. New York: New York University Press, 1998.

Meyer, Leisa D. Creating GI Jane. Sexuality and Power in the Women's Army Corps During World War II. New York: Columbia University Press, 1996.

Miller, Grace Porter. Call of Duty. A Montana Girl in World War II. Baton Rouge: Louisiana State University Press, 1999.

Military Service Publishing Company. The Officer's Guide. Harrisburg: The Military Service Publishing Company, 1943.

Morden, Bettie J. The Women's Army Corps 1945-1978. Washington, D.C.: U.S. Government Printing Office, 1989.

Schaffer, Mollie Weinstein with Schaffer, Cyndee. Mollie's War. Jefferson, NC: McFarland & Company, Inc., 2010.

Starbird, Ethel A. When Women First Wore Army Shoes. New York: IUniverse, Inc., 2010.

Treadwell, Mattie E. U.S. Army in World War II Special Studies. The Women's Army Corps. Washington, D.C., Office of the Chief of Military History. Department of the Army: 1954.

U.S. Army. The Women's Army Corps in World War II. Washington, D.C.: U.S. Government Printing Office, undated.

Williams, Vera S. WACs Women's Army Corps. Osceola, WI: 1997.

# Index

Air Corps Advanced Flying School 31
American Volunteer Group 31, 33, 148
Army Air Forces School of Applied Tactics 36

Bennett, Elsie 118
Bethlehem 91
Brouk, Emily 29
Brouk, Harold 29
Brouk, Peter 29
Brouk, Robert 7, 13, 14, 29, 30, 31, 32, 33, 34, 35, 36, 37, 38, 39, 40, 41, 42, 48, 49, 68, 69, 118, 132, 133
Brouk, Virginia 37, 38, 39, 40,. 41, 42, 48, 49, 53, 55, 57, 58, 59, 60, 61, 63, 64, 66, 67, 68, 69, 71, 72, 73, 76, 118, 119

Camp Huckstep 82, 83, 87, 129
Camp Patrick Henry 72, 73
Central Aircraft Manufacturing Company 31, 32
Chennault, Claire Lee 31
Chicago, Illlinois 9, 16, 17, 22, 29, 30, 33, 36, 37, 39, 41, 48, 49, 100, 101, 113, 118, 119, 121, 129, 130
Chinese Air Force 31
Church of All Nations 93
Cyprus 117, 122, 124, 125, 127, 128

Davis, Everett 118
Davis, Fred 7, 14, 118, 119, 121, 133
George, George 118
Davis, Harvey 7, 118, 119, 120
Davis, Robert 118
Davis, Virginia
Dyer, Major Josephine 82

Egypt 79, 83, 87, 94, 95, 100, 101, 102, 105, 107, 108, 112, 114, 115, 122, 125, 129, 132
　Alexandria 79, 108
　Cairo 78, 82, 83, 84, 86, 87, 88, 108, 109, 110, 112, 114, 115, 122, 123, 128, 129
　Devesior 119
　Payne Field 122, 129

Florida
　Kissimmee 38
　Orlando 36
Flying Tigers 32, 33, 41, 131, 148
Frillman, Reverend Paul 35

Garden of Gethsemane 93
Georgria
　Ft. Oglethorpe 49

Hawaii, Pearl Harbor 32, 58, 59, 148
Hello Charley 19, 20, 21, 22, 26, 27, 32, 34, 40, 48, 51, 104
Hobby, Oveta Culp 45, 49

Illinois
    Chicago, 9, 16, 17, 22, 29, 30, 33, 36, 37, 39, 41, 48, 49, 100, 101, 113, 118, 119, 121, 129, 130
    Evanston 16
    Oak Park 29
Iowa
    Fort Des Moines 45, 59, 130
Isle of Capri 81
Italy
    Bagnoli 73, 75
    Casino 81
    Mt. Vesuvius 78, 81
    Naples 75, 78, 79, 80
    Pompeii 78, 80, 81
    Rome 75, 79, 125
    Salerno 79, 81

Jefferson County Orphan Asylum 118
Jerusalem 91, 92, 93
Jones, Reverend William 130

Kane, Sidney O. 38

Langford, Lt. Paul 68, 69
Lewis Institute of Technology 31

Madame Chiang Kai-Shek 41
Morton High School 29, 34
Morton Junior College 29, 30, 31
Mount Olive 93

New York
    Mitchel Field 31

Ohio
    Patterson Field 130

Palestine 89, 90, 94

Scharer, Frieda 16, 17
Scharer, Oscar 16, 17
Scharer, Ruth 16, 17
Scharer, Virginia 16, 17, 18, 19,, 20, 21, 22, 23, 28, 29, 32, 33, 34

Shaffer, Major Oliver 55
Steinmetz High School 17
Suez Canal 89

Texas
    Kelly Field 31
The Citadel 93

Utah
    Fort Douglas 50
    Provo 53, 57, 68, 69
    Salt Lake City 51, 55, 63, 64, 69

Vera Janes Studios 17

Watertown, New York 118
Western Electric 17, 18, 19, 20, 21, 27, 33, 34, 35, 61
Women's Army Corps 13, 49, 53, 55, 56, 58, 59, 63, 68, 79
Woodrow Wilson Grammar School 29
Wyoming
    Fort Warren, 29

# About The Author

## About The Author

Jennifer is a genealogical, historical, and military researcher. She lectures throughout the Chicagoland area on World War II records and stories, kids genealogy, and Italian genealogy.

As a researcher and writer she can help you research and piece together the stories of your ancestors, particularly if they served during World War II.

She is on the staff of the World War II History Network. You can join the community at http://wwiihistorynetwork.com

Jennifer volunteers as the Genealogy Department Manager at Casa Italia in Stone Park, Illinois. There she hosts monthly genealogy and writing programs and works in the Italian American Veterans Museum.

You can learn more about Jennifer and utilitze her World War II Researcher's Toolbox at http://jenniferholik.com

## Coming Winter 2015!

Volume 1 of *Stories from The Battlefield,* a new 4-volume book series that will help you navigate World War II military records. Sign up for my newsletter at http://jenniferholik.com to stay in touch and receive details about these books, pre-sales, special offers, and tips on researching and writing your military ancestor stories.

## Books By Author

All books and associated guides can be purchased through the author's website or on Amazon.com

*Stories from the Battlefield: A Beginning Guide to World War II Records*  **Release Date: August 2014**

All the records burned! We hear this over and over when we think about World War II research. Yet there are many records and resources available to get you started. In this short guide, you will learn the basics of World War II military research and what to look for in your home sources. Then we will explore components of personnel files, death records, and other associated records in this short book.

This guide is meant to be a starting point for World War II research, not an exhaustive examination of all the military branches and records available. In 2015 I will release the first in a series of in-depth books on World War II records, the first being Stories from the Battlefield Volume I: Navigating World War II Home Front, Civilian, Army, and Air Corps Records. Please visit my website for more details on the release dates.

*Stories of the Lost*

Imagine sending your son off to war. Will he return unharmed, unchanged, and whole? How long will he be gone? Will the war last forever? Will he return? Standing in front of you at the railroad station is a young man in uniform. He looks so handsome, so strong, and full of life. You hug him tightly before he boards the train. You wave goodbye and he's gone.

Years later your son returns from the war. He arrives not walking off the train, but carried off in a flag draped casket. Dead almost four years now and buried in a foreign land, you did not know where he was buried for almost two years after he was killed. Your son is unable to tell his story of war. Who will tell his story?

This book is a collection of stories about my relatives who left by train to fight for our freedom and never returned. Three of the men were brought home after the war ended. One however, still sleeps in that foreign soil. It is also the recognition of the men who cared for them after death. The stories of the lost found through the military record.

*To Soar with the Tigers*

This is the story of Flying Tiger Robert Brouk, a Flight Leader in the 3rd Squadron of the American Volunteer Group. In the months prior to Pearl Harbor, until the disbandment of the American Volunteer Group in July 1942, the Flying Tigers valiantly fought the Japanese over the skies of Burma and China. This story contains Robert's complete war diary. The diary outlines his dramatic experiences from the moment he enlisted in the American Volunteer Group to its disbandment. His story also contains snapshots of the life he led upon his return to his home in Cicero, Illinois; a graphic account of his untimely death; and accounts of how Robert has been remembered through the years.

*Branching Out: Genealogy for Students 1st-3rd Grade*
*Branching Out: Genealogy for Students 4th-8th Grade*
*Branching Out: Genealogy for High School Students*
*Branching Out: Genealogy for Adults*

Are you looking for a how-to genealogy book that introduces the basics of research through easy to learn lessons? Then look no further. In Branching Out, a new series available from Generations, author and professional genealogist Jennifer Holik provides adults with the tools they need to learn how to research their family history. Through thirty fun and educational lessons, you will learn the foundations of genealogy and how to begin research. Each lesson contains a clearly defined goal, all necessary vocabulary, additional reading assignments, and lesson and homework assignments to extend understanding of the concept.

*Engaging the Next Generation: A Guide for Genealogy Societies and Libraries*

Engaging the Next Generation is written specifically for groups looking to create youth programs. This is a two-part book featuring one-hour and half-day youth program examples and the complete 4th-8th grade Branching Out set of thirty lessons. Part I allows genealogy societies and libraries to create youth programs based on example outlines, example speaking text, and project ideas in the book. Part II allows genealogy societies and libraries to build larger programs using the thirty lessons provided in the Branching Out series. Part II can also be used to teach beginning genealogy in public schools.

Made in the USA
Charleston, SC
11 July 2014